SUCCESS THROUGH LESS

Praise for Rolf Dobelli

'I don't just read Rolf Dobelli's books; I savour every word.' *Frank Elstner, German TV host*

'One of Europe's finest minds.' *Matt Ridley, bestselling author*

'Rolf Dobelli is a virtuosic synthesizer of ideas. With wit, grace and precision, he melds science and art in his joyful pursuit of wisdom.' *Joshua Greene, Professor of Psychology, Harvard University, and author of* Moral Tribes

'Rolf Dobelli has a gift for identifying the best ideas in the world and then putting them together in ways that make the whole even more valuable than the sum of the parts. He's done it for the art of thinking. Now he does it for the art of living.' *Jonathan Haidt, Professor of Ethical Leadership, NYU Stern School of Business, and the* New York Times-*bestselling author of* The Righteous Mind

'Rolf Dobelli is brilliant at converting evidence from scientific research into practical steps that improve personal outcomes.' *Robert B. Cialdini, author of bestsellers* Influence *and* Pre-Suasion

'Rolf Dobelli has done it again! Not only does he open our eyes, now he wakes us up. Because of his rigorous scientific analysis combined with his shattering philosophical approach, he is never satisfied with the superficial. So, grab Rolf's book and don't let it go!' *Tenley E. Albright, Director, MIT Collaborative Initiatives, and Professor Emeritus, Harvard Medical School*

'Rolf Dobelli gives us as valuable advice about how to live as he did about how to think.' *James R. Flynn, Professor Emeritus, University of Otago, and discoverer of the Flynn Effect*

'Rolf Dobelli possesses the fascinating knack to present modern scientific insights in an inspiring and thrilling way.' *Bruno S. Frey, Professor of Economics, University of Basel, and founder of the field of economic happiness research*

'Three pages in, and you've already learned something else.' *Franz Himpsel*, Süddeutsche Zeitung

'This book will change the way you think.' *Professor Dan Goldstein, London Business School*

'This book provides a truly fresh perspective. It is intelligent, informative and witty. Rolf Dobelli's clear prose illuminates how we think.' *Dr Christoph Franz, former CEO, Lufthansa; Global Chairman, Roche*

'Do you have to read this book? Definitely. It's extremely entertaining and offers a fundamentally sound introduction to the nature of human thought.' *Professor Dr (h. c.) Roland Berger, Founder and Honorary Chairman of Roland Berger Strategy Consultants*

'Brimming with insights! Anybody who's sick of constantly stumbling into mental traps has got to read this book.' *Professor Iris Bohnet, Harvard Kennedy School*

SUCCESS THROUGH LESS

THE 52 HABITS STANDING BETWEEN YOU AND YOUR BEST LIFE

ROLF DOBELLI

Translated from the German by Isabel Adey

ALLEN&UNWIN

Originally published in Germany in 2024 by Piper Verlag GmbH, München / Berlin.

First published as *The Not-To-Do List* in hardback and trade paperback in
Great Britain in 2025 by Allen & Unwin, an imprint of Atlantic Books Ltd.

This paperback edition published in 2026 by Allen & Unwin.

10 9 8 7 6 5 4 3 2 1

A CIP catalogue record for this book is available from the British Library.

Paperback ISBN: 978 1 80546 330 6
E-book ISBN: 978 1 80546 329 0

Printed and bound by CPI (UK) Ltd, Croydon CR0 4YY

Allen & Unwin
An imprint of Atlantic Books Ltd
Ormond House
26–27 Boswell Street
London
WC1N 3JZ

www.atlantic-books.co.uk

Product safety EU representative: Authorised Rep Compliance Ltd., Ground Floor,
71 Lower Baggot Street, Dublin, D02 P593, Ireland. www.arccompliance.com

CONTENTS

CONTENTS

For my wife Clara Maria Bagus and our sons

FOREWORD

Some people collect vinyl, video game consoles or vintage clothes. For years, I've been accumulating stories of failure – botched attempts at work, family life, marriage and life in general.

Leo Tolstoy's monumental novel *Anna Karenina* opens with the line 'Happy families are all alike; every unhappy family is unhappy in its own way.' Meaning: unadulterated joy makes for a dull read. Happiness is bland and one-dimensional, smooth like Teflon. Unhappiness, on the other hand, tells us more about the world. Misery is textured. And it teaches us lessons. That's why I'm an avid collector of woe and misfortune.

On graduation day, colleges and universities invite a guest speaker to share their insights and wisdom with the fledglings being released into the world of work. These speakers are usually former students of the institution who have excelled in their chosen career. This was the case on 13 June 1986, when Charlie Munger, then aged 62, was invited to deliver the commencement speech at the Harvard School in Los Angeles. The American investor, together with Warren Buffett, had built arguably the most successful holding company in history: Berkshire Hathaway. Munger's speech was most extraordinary. Even the title had a bizarre ring to it: 'How to Guarantee a Life of Misery'. Instead of imparting insights to help his audience achieve better personal outcomes, he shared four failsafe ways to achieve zero success in life. He simply flipped the whole thing on its head. It was a brilliant stroke of inspiration; after all, negative rules are more powerful than their positive counterparts, more concrete and memorable. Despite all the research into happiness, for example, we still don't know exactly what makes us happy. We certainly know what destroys happiness, though. We can't pinpoint what leads to success, but we know for sure what makes it an impossibility. The key is to keep the killer in your sights and give him the slip, then the right path will automatically open up ahead.

Munger's idea was by no means new. The Prussian mathematician Carl Gustav Jacobi applied this approach back in the nineteenth century. Sometimes, he realized, the only way to solve an academic problem is to turn it around completely. The technical term is 'inversion'. This is what led Einstein to adapt Newton's theory of gravity to Maxwell's electromagnetism, instead of approaching the problem the other way round like everyone else had done before him. Long-term investors ask themselves how best to run a company into the ground, then they invest in indestructible prospects. Munger's witty one-liner sums up this approach perfectly: 'All I want to know is where I'm going to die, so I'll never go there.' In addition to being a brilliant investor, Charlie Munger was an equally ingenious thinker who was never one to hold back. As the source of so many incisive remarks, he is someone I quote often. He sadly passed away at the age of 99 while I was writing this book.

Back to the subject at hand: inversion. We tend to dissect successes, but not failures, in our own life or in the media. There is an additional bias here: in the case of success, we systematically overestimate the role of skills, decisions and actions, and underestimate the role of chance, luck, randomness. Why? Because we hear about successful companies, projects and people in the media. Flops, on the other hand – no one wants to know about them. Deadbeats don't usually write autobiographies. And in the rare event that they do, they fail to find a publisher, let alone an audience. So we study these shining examples and delude ourselves into thinking that achievements are the result of a series of carefully orchestrated success factors, when really what matters is steering clear of common pitfalls. Tip: visit the graveyards of failed companies, projects, people, marriages and families. That's where you'll learn the most – namely, what to avoid.

Of the twelve books I've written, three were major successes and a handful were veritable flops. I have no idea what made *The*

Art of Thinking Clearly an international bestseller, but I know exactly where the others went wrong. If you view the world from a negative perspective, you bring light into the darkness.

My previous books employed the same approach as the conventional graduation speech. They offer advice on how to think clearly, act wisely and live a better life. But in this book, I'm turning the tables. I give you a whole catalogue of habits, behaviours and thought patterns that are best avoided – a 'not-to-do list', if you will, a sort of encyclopaedia of foolishness, a taxonomy of the habits that stand between you and your best self. Some of them may even remind you of advice you've encountered from celebrity life coaches, self-help gurus or online influencers. If you know what they are, you can also steer clear of them: success through less. Each chapter then offers, as an antidote, a gentle word from the quiet voice of reason.

My sons were in the back of my mind the whole time I was writing this book. One day, when they're fully grown, I picture myself handing them a copy and saying, 'Hopefully this will spare you a few problems in life. If you avoid these 52 things, you can look forward to a bright future.' No doubt they'll just laugh at me and say, 'That's nice of you, Dad, but we were really hoping for a car or some money for a round-the-world trip!'

Rolf Dobelli

1

LET THINGS FALL APART

There once was a man who lived in an old house with a leaky roof. It was never the right time to fix the roof: when it rained it was too wet, and when the skies were clear he saw no need. If you want to do badly in life, follow the old man's example. Systematically neglect the upkeep of your house, your car, your body, your mind, your relationships, your business – your entire life. It's the only way to guarantee that it'll all go to pieces.

The quiet voice of reason

On a stormy Tuesday in August 2018, the Morandi Bridge in Genoa collapsed. It had been completed in 1967 and formed part of a major arterial road linking the Italian Riviera with the French coast. Designed by Italian engineer Riccardo Morandi, the viaduct was innovative in its construction: three reinforced concrete pylons supporting several pre-stressed concrete stays. Long before it collapsed, experts had voiced concerns about the corrosion of the concrete and these structural elements. No remedial action was taken. When the middle section of the bridge gave way, dozens of cars plummeted 40 metres to the ground. A frantic rescue operation immediately ensued in a desperate bid to help the survivors and recover the bodies. In a remarkable feat, the bridge was speedily rebuilt and reopened in August 2020. The heroic rescuers and star architect Renzo Piano, who rebuilt the bridge, were celebrated for their efforts.

On 14 August 2018, that same stormy Tuesday, the Felsenau Viaduct in Bern did not collapse. Completed in 1974 and located just a few kilometres from my office, this particular bridge forms part of Switzerland's A1 motorway, our country's most important transport axis. It is comparable to the Morandi Bridge in Genoa in terms of age, construction, materials, length and traffic volume. But here in Bern, no one was celebrated. There is no monument to the specialists responsible for the ongoing maintenance of the bridge; they received no medals for their work, not even an article in the local newspaper.

Maintenance is by no means a heroic deed. It is boring and unsexy, and most of it goes unseen. But that's not to say it's any less important than heroism – in fact, quite the opposite. While we systematically overestimate the value of a grand design or a brave rescue mission, we systematically underestimate the value of quiet ongoing maintenance. Not just on public buildings, but also in the private sphere. We heap praise on the surgeon who saved us from a fatal heart attack, but not the GP we regularly visit for check-ups, even though those check-ups have kept us from dying of bowel cancer thus far. We glorify the moment when our Mr or Mrs Right proposed to us, but we underestimate the value of the monotonous, time-devouring daily maintenance of the relationship. As the German comedian Hape Kerkeling says, 'Love is work, work, work.'

The maintenance people of the business world get overlooked, too. Company founders and turnaround CEOS are applauded. But who celebrates the millions of middle managers who keep thousands of business operations, data centres, power grids and warehouses up and running – everything through to waste removal? David Brooks, a columnist for the *New York Times*, rightly describes these invisible middle managers as 'the unsung heroes of our age'. Still, no one writes about them.

In geopolitics, the true heroes are not the generals who lead an army (and their country) to victory. The real heroes are the individuals who prevent a war from happening in the first place: the politicians, diplomats and civil servants who keep the international lines of communication open and establish an effective deterrent. But are diplomats rewarded for wars that never take place? Does anyone read their memoirs?

Bottom line: there are no medals to be won for diligent maintenance. That being said, this kind of work is still more important than any other. My advice for a good life: don't wait for things to fall apart. Remain careful and watchful – like the engineers entrusted with the upkeep of state-of-the-art jet engines. As well as carrying out continuous maintenance work, they rely on sophisticated performance monitoring processes. In the event of even the tiniest fluctuation (temperature, pressure, vibration) from the normal range, the plane is immediately taken out of service until the issue has been rectified. You should get into a similar habit. Are you finding it harder to get up the stairs these days? Then make an appointment with your doctor. Is your husband or wife chronically irritable? Have a conversation, find out what's bothering them. Is there woodworm in your roof beams? Call a specialist before the roof caves in on you. Better to be an unsung hero than someone who tries to save the day and fails dramatically.

SEE ALSO **Drink Yourself Miserable** (ch. 12); **Only Learn from Your Own Experience** (ch. 14); **Get Rich Quick, Get Smart Quick** (ch. 35); **Do Only Shallow Work** (ch. 47)

2

FEED YOUR WEAKER SELF

There's an epidemic of self-discipline happening. Every other self-help book preaches self-motivation, with titles like *The Mountain is You* and *Discipline: the Power of Self-Control* regularly featuring on the bestseller lists. Beware: don't let this pseudo-religion sink its teeth into you. These writers just want to make money. If you can't be bothered doing something, your central nervous system is clearly trying to tell you that it couldn't possibly be worth your while. Why else would human beings have developed this complex feeling over millions of years of evolution? Trust your inner sloth; he's your loyal companion. If he squeaks, stroke his head, ruffle his fur and give him a couple of treats.

Motivation has to come from the outside, not – as these authors would all have you believe – from within. It's not your fault if you're in the doldrums; the world en masse is to blame. Unless the universe gives you a reason to get out of bed and deal with all the irksome things in life, what else are you supposed to do? That's right: just stay in bed. Self-motivation is about as natural as plastic or pesticides. Consider how animals behave in their natural habitat. Gorillas, for example: they just sit around scratching themselves and digesting food. Stress and bad moods? Not a chance. We share 98 per cent of our genes with gorillas, so we should really be looking to them to lead the way. Advocates of strict discipline have forgotten what comes naturally to us. Disinclination is disinclination – our evolutionary forebears knew that much.

Here's a new motto for you to live by: put off till tomorrow what you can do today. Ideally you should get together with a whole mob of like-minded people and collectively deride the excesses of self-motivation. Maybe you could even start an international procrastination movement? Actually, maybe not – that would take up too much of your time.

The quiet voice of reason

The German-speaking world has a great term for this weaker self: *innere Schweinehund*, which literally means 'inner pigdog'. A bit like a sloth, but with malicious intent. This creature made its way into common parlance after World War II, when gym teachers would yell at the top of their voices and urge their students to conquer the slovenly creature, i.e., to overcome their innate idleness by force of discipline and willpower. It's an evolutionary fact that we all have our own pigdog dwelling within us. In hunter-gatherer communities, it was counterproductive to use one's energy for anything other than survival. Highly motivated individuals who roused themselves for non-essential activities burned valuable calories, leaving them with a deficit when the next famine hit. Their genes consequently disappeared from the gene pool, which makes us the successors of the undermotivated survivors.

Our ancestors were perfectly active when it came to hunger, danger or mating. But once their bellies were full, lazing around was the most rational thing for them to do. They didn't have freezers where they could store excess game, or bank accounts where they could deposit surplus berries. Other people's bodies were the only answer to a fridge. In those days, if you killed a bison, you wouldn't be advised to gorge on it and leave the scraps for the hyenas. No, you'd do well to be generous and share the meat with your kin – preferably with the neighbouring tribes, too. That way, if the gods of hunting failed to smile on you for a few days, you'd at least be able to rely on others for food.

Nowadays, however, the demands we face are exactly the opposite. We've created an entire infrastructure of accumulation – everything from warehouses to pension funds, performance records, technological expertise, publications and social media likes. Almost everything we do and consume can be amassed and accumulated for later use. But what happens when our inner pigdog suddenly appears, blocking our path? How do we turn a deaf ear to his whimpering?

Self-motivation is like a muscle. If you overexert yourself, the muscle will get tired and you'll find your willpower waning. But by making demands on that muscle, you are simultaneously training it. As the months and years go by, your willpower will grow and you'll find it increasingly easy to conquer your inner pigdog. Self-motivation might be strenuous, but it is learnable.

One thing that doesn't work particularly well, though, is trying to motivate other people. You can use the carrot-and-stick approach (in other words, incentives) to spur on your significant other, children or staff, but this is *not* the same as motivation. You see, true motivation can only come from within. If, as the one in charge, you have to motivate your staff, the fact is that you're already fighting a losing battle. It makes much more sense to employ highly motivated individuals from the get-go – and to be one, too. Incidentally: if you happen to have bagged yourself an apathetic life partner, it's wiser to get a divorce than to try to motivate them.

SEE ALSO **Cling to Your Bad Habits** (ch. 10); **Feel Guilty** (ch. 22); **Live in the Past** (ch. 27); **Let Your Emotions Define You** (ch. 39); **Try to Change People** (ch. 44); **Spin Multiple Plates** (ch. 46)

3

BE UNRELIABLE

The Germans have a saying: *'Ist der Ruf erst ruiniert, lebt es sich ganz ungeniert.'* Roughly translated, it means 'Once your reputation is in tatters, how you live doesn't matter.' If you want to live a deeply unhappy life, the imminent ruin of your reputation should be one of your top priorities. Rule one: never keep your promises! If you want to be excluded from all the most important circles, complete unreliability is the main trait you need. As the American investor Charlie Munger said in his commencement address at the Harvard School in Los Angeles, 'First, be unreliable ... If you will only master this one habit, you will more than counterbalance the combined effect of all your virtues, howsoever great.'

I recommend taking this unreliability to the next level. Instead of just failing to deliver what can be reasonably expected of you, why not promise the moon and the stars, then immediately forget all about it. Over time, you won't even have to make promises any more. Everyone will already know to expect nothing but hot air from you. People will let themselves be fooled once, maybe twice. Then they'll be through with you. As a seasoned fraud, you'll just have to keep finding new victims. Eventually this may prove difficult, because people are bound to talk. You'll become the subject of gossip; your reputation will go down the drain, and for the rest of your life that's where it'll stay. Take my advice: treat your promises like toilet paper.

The quiet voice of reason

I'm constantly amazed at what people can achieve by being reliable, even if they don't have an exceptional IQ and aren't particularly creative. When it comes to success, reliability is the most underrated factor at play. In fact, I think it's the most powerful tool there is. Intellectual brilliance won't save you from falling flat on your face. Think about the collapse of the Long-Term Capital Management hedge fund in 1998. Every single member of the management team had an exceptionally high IQ; two were even Nobel Prize winners. Creativity, athleticism and charisma are no guarantee of success either. Reliability, on the other hand, is. If you're reliable, you don't have to worry about falling, because there's no web of lies waiting to unravel beneath your feet. Even if your IQ is sky-high or you're a galactic talent, why not top it off by being reliable to boot? It won't cost a thing. Yes, all the brilliant, creative people I know – from big-name architects to Nobel Prize winners and world-class musicians – are extremely reliable. That doesn't make them any less cool; quite the opposite. Being unreliable is what's uncool.

The eighteenth-century Scottish moral philosopher Adam Smith, known as the father of modern economics, attributed prosperity to the division of labour. The role of innovation came later. But again, here in the economic arena, the secret key to success (reliability) is often overlooked. Eight billion consumers on the planet, a hundred million companies, ten million different products, trillions of goods flows. None of this would be possible without exceptional reliability. On a large scale, contracts are what regulate reliability. If a company fails to deliver on time or if the quality is lacking, they may face legal action. But on a smaller scale, reliability is a matter of reputation. And in the digital age, reputations are easily tarnished. It takes ten years to build a reputation, but just ten seconds to ruin it.

In the old days, when someone squandered their reputation, they could just move to another city and start again. Not any more. You can only gamble away your reputation once. In financial terms, your reliability's worth is the 'total discounted cash flow' of the rest of your professional life. Go on, do the maths – we're soon talking millions here. Small emotional perk: it's not only better for everyone else if you're reliable; it's also better for you. The satisfaction of keeping your word is one of the best feelings there is. Being unreliable belongs firmly on your not-to-do list.

SEE ALSO **Listen to Your Inner Voice** (ch. 28); **Trade Your Reputation for Money** (ch. 37); **Say Everything You Think** (ch. 45); **Say Yes to Everything** (ch. 50)

4

BE AN ASSHOLE

Are you already known for your arrogance? Excellent. Then go on, crank it up a notch. Act like an asshole; it's the quickest route to a miserable life. This works particularly well if your name isn't Aristotle and you've never won a Nobel Prize. But other than that, it doesn't matter whether you're rich or poor, important or a nobody, beautiful or ugly – an ass is still an ass. If you want to reach peak asshole, take my advice: when other people are talking, don't listen to a word – you already know much better than them. If someone gives you feedback, tell them to take a look in the mirror. Never practise gratitude. Make it clear that you'd have made it to exactly where you are without any help from those around you. When working in a team, never let others share in your glory. But do be sure to pass the buck any time things go wrong. It can't have anything to do with you now, can it?

Celebrate your colossal ego. Have your photo taken by a hotshot photographer and flaunt the images on your office wall. Be your own biggest fan – that way, you can be sure there'll always be someone who likes you. Get some little statues of yourself made. It's no longer rocket science, thanks to 3D printers. Proudly place one on your desk. If anyone asks, you can always pretend it's meant to be ironic. The others make for great gifts if you've run out of self-penned books to give away.

Pay attention to your tone of voice and your body language, making sure they're both as condescending as possible. When communicating, it's important to always show a degree of disrespect. The odd snide remark here and there should do the trick. Banging on about your legendary successes isn't enough. I also recommend boasting wildly about even your smallest wins. Never put yourself in anyone else's shoes; only ever wear your own. But do demand that other people put themselves in your position in order to better understand where you're coming from. Whether you achieve great things or minuscule triumphs, remain immodest. Remember that success is always down to your absolute competence, whereas failure is always caused by factors beyond your control. And finally: only ever offer your support if you clearly stand to gain something in return.

Charlie Munger tells the story of a priest who called upon mourners at a funeral to say something nice about the deceased. No one came forward. After a very long time, one guy stood up and said, 'His brother was worse.' There's a lesson to be learned from this anecdote. Your aim in life should be for people to attend your funeral for just one reason: to make sure that you're really dead.

The quiet voice of reason

Arrogance is easy. Modesty is tough, especially when we've accomplished something. As human beings, we experience our own achievements more intensely. This means we tend to give them too much weight, which is why arrogance often follows hot on the heels of success. I arrived late when God was handing out the virtue of modesty, so I had to acquire it rationally. If we're being logical, success is merely the final link in a long chain of coincidences for which we ourselves can take zero credit. So if you really think about it, there's nothing for us to be proud of.

Moreover, almost all human achievements are the result of cooperation. Alone we achieve nothing, but together we can do almost anything. Look around you. What do you see? Books, pens, shoes, windows, bulbs, smartphones, wall paint? Not one of these things was made by one person alone. Not even you are your own creation; were it not for thousands upon thousands of ancestors, you wouldn't exist. In short: everything you achieve, you do so with the help of other people, some of whom you know, most of whom you've never met. It follows that showing modesty, kindness, gratitude and appreciation is not only tactically advantageous but in fact a sensible, authentic way to live.

The Mayo Clinic is the leading hospital chain in the United States. At every interview – from secretary to star surgeon – the team adds up the instances of the words 'I' and 'we' in the candidate's responses. If the word 'I' comes out on top, it's a strong indicator that they aren't a team player and won't be the right fit for the hospital. Main takeaway: the smaller your ego, the better your life will be. And yes, if you're an asshole, you deserve to be treated like one.

SEE ALSO **Be Hypocritical** (ch. 9); **Make Other People Feel Unimportant** (ch. 26); **Cultivate a Victim Mentality** (ch. 33); **Try to End It All** (ch. 40); **Say Everything You Think** (ch. 45)

5

HAVE HIGH EXPECTATIONS

Have high expectations of yourself and of others. This golden path to a miserable life is always the way to go. When the US investor Warren Buffet was asked for his secret to a solid marriage (his first lasted 52 years and his second is still going strong), he didn't simply reel off a list of desirable qualities to look for in a partner, like beauty, intelligence, diligence, competence and emotional stability. Instead, he talked about the importance of having 'low expectations' in a relationship. Low expectations, he said, are the best way to guarantee a long, happy partnership. So if you want to royally screw up your relationship, make sure that you hold your significant other to the very highest standards. Even more importantly, make sure that your partner sets extremely high expectations for you, too. Your marriage will go down in the history books – as the shortest on record.

This rule doesn't just apply to marriages. The more you expect of anything in life – a book, a film, a friend, the government, your health, human progress or simply the day ahead – the greater your disappointment will be. Got kids? If so, set the bar as high as you humanly can, especially while they're still in nappies. It's hardly likely that you've spawned your very own Leonardo da Vinci or Maria Sklodowska – later Marie Curie, who went on to be awarded two Nobel Prizes. The chances of this are extremely slim, so it follows that your kids are bound to disappoint you. Not only that, but they'll sense your disappointment, too. Follow this rule in their early years to lay the foundations for a tumultuous relationship that's sure to be beyond repair by the time they hit puberty (if not before).

The quiet voice of reason

Your brain generates expectations, whether you want it to or not. Most scientists assume that it operates according to the Bayesian method, named after the eighteenth-century English mathematician Thomas Bayes. This is how it works: the brain hypothesizes that a particular event has a particular likelihood of occurring. However, this probability is constantly being adjusted based on information from new experiences – a bit like software updates on your laptop.

For example: you expect water to gush from the cistern when you flush the toilet. After a few repetitions, your brain registers that this happens almost every time, so it calculates an accurate probability of somewhere between 99 and 100 per cent. Of course, it's much more difficult with things that rarely happen or might even be happening for the first time. Like the first time you sleep with someone, go to university, have a child, change jobs, start a new business or jet off on a round-the-world trip. In these cases, your brain doesn't have access to prior knowledge of incidence gained from experience. So it makes a guess based on hopes, which by definition are higher than they should be; if not, they wouldn't be hopes.

If you have your sights set on a life of contentment, I recommend the following course of action before embarking on any new experience. Rate your hopes on a scale of 0 (epic failure) to 10 (sky-high satisfaction). Then deliberately deduct three points. If you do this, you'll save yourself a whole load of disappointment. Not only that, but you'll also get a nice surprise on those odd occasions when reality exceeds your low expectations. Here's the most important bit: make sure that the people closest to you (your life partner, for example) manage their expectations of you, too. Sure, this can be tricky; it's not like you can get inside their heads and start interfering with their brains. But you can be real with them from the start. What I mean is, don't put on an act on your first date. Behave like the person you really are (and will presumably continue to be for the rest of your life). You don't have to come across as a blithering idiot to curb expectations, but you should definitely let your bad attributes shine through. Like it or not, after just a few months – if the relationship lasts that long – your partner's 'Bayesian brain' will more or less have the measure of you anyway.

If your partner does eventually decide to marry you, I recommend reading novels together. And no, I'm not talking about those novels with sparkly covers, the ones you can buy in supermarkets, but literature, great literature. After all, most of it is about broken relationships. Maybe the contrast will make your partner seem like a fairy-tale prince or princess after all.

SEE ALSO **Mess Up Your Marriage** (ch. 7); **Be Hyperactive on Social Media** (ch. 15); **Trust Your Banker** (ch. 24); **Expect Rationality** (ch. 29); **Join a Cult** (ch. 43); **Crowd Your Life with Gadgets** (ch. 51)

6

DRIFT THROUGH THE DAY

Have you planned the day ahead down to the very last detail? Why bother? Do you really want to achieve quite so much? Think of the items on your to-do list as wishes, a flutter of hope, an optional, moveable feast. Write lists not for yourself, but for a fairy godmother who might just come along and check them off for you. And anyway, even if she doesn't, what difference does it make? Plans will only make you feel under pressure. Your best bet is to give them a miss.

The brain is designed for spontaneity, so it's better to keep yourself open to chance. If you wander aimlessly through the world, it's sure to spit out a steady stream of inspiration for you to soak up. Planning your day – in fact, planning in general – is fundamentally unnatural. We're not evolutionarily prepared for it. I mean, can you remember ever hearing about archaeologists unearthing a to-do list on a prehistoric dig?

A fully planned day removes any opportunity for creativity. Like a lid on a flame, those plans will only stifle your sparking ideas. True, 99.9 per cent of your ideas deserve to be smothered, but the probability of a stroke of genius is still higher than zero. Who knows, maybe this very one tenth of a per cent will be the inspiration for an international bestseller? Or maybe even a solution for saving the planet?

Another thing: time management is time-consuming. Think of all the things you could have accomplished while you were busy making plans – like checking out special offers on Amazon or posting pictures of your breakfast on Instagram. So if a pitiful life is what you're after, be sure to give planning a wide berth!

The quiet voice of reason

Successful people give themselves orders. Entrepreneurs set aside two hours in the morning to go through their mailing list and call potential customers, even though they'd much prefer to be deep in conversation with ChatGPT. Writers give themselves a six-hour block and sit down to work, even when they're really not in the mood. The American author Julia Alvarez once confessed, 'If I had to wake up every morning and decide if I felt like writing, nine times out of ten, I wouldn't feel like it.' In short, writing is a battle. It's the same for all the writers I know. General Eisenhower famously said, 'I gave myself an order.' An order that he set his mind to and treated like a command from a superior officer.

Resistance: futile.

About 150 years ago, a man walked up to John Pierpont (J. P.) Morgan, the richest man in the world at the time. He held up an envelope and said, 'Sir, in my hand I hold a guaranteed formula for success, which I will gladly sell you for $25,000.' (That's roughly half a million dollars in today's terms.) To this, Morgan replied, 'Sir, I do not know what is in the envelope; however, if you show me, and I like it, I give you my word as a gentleman that I will pay you what you ask.' The man gave him the envelope, which Morgan proceeded to open. He took out a piece of paper and paid the man the $25,000 as agreed. On the sheet of paper were the words: 'Every morning, write a list of the things that need to be done that day. Do them.'

I can't think of a single successful person I know who doesn't plan their day in blocks of an hour or thirty minutes. Open-ended to-do lists aren't good enough. Incorporate the items on your list into your daily routine; treat them as if they were important meetings (with yourself). This will force you to estimate how many blocks of time each individual task requires, how many tasks will fit into a day, and which you should tackle in the morning when your brain is still fresh (i.e., the most demanding ones).

The only issue with detailed planning is that most people take on too much. We're notoriously overoptimistic about what we can achieve with our time. That's not such a bad thing, though. The key is to follow your own orders and stick to the roadmap, even if it doesn't work out perfectly.

Anything that's left to deal with, you can set aside for a specific point in time, preferably the next morning. Then you can wake up, look in the mirror and say to yourself, 'At your command!'

SEE ALSO **Set the Wrong Goals** (ch. 11); **Catastrophize** (ch. 31); **Do Only Shallow Work** (ch. 47); **Say Yes to Everything** (ch. 50)

7

MESS UP YOUR MARRIAGE

If your marriage is basically healthy but you're hell-bent on screwing it up, here are some pointers to bear in mind.

When it comes to criticism, never hold back! The completely useless object that your partner picked up from one of those pointless stores and that's now occupying the last patch of space left in your home: what the hell? The wild proliferation of lamps, tealights, candles, houseplants, little tins and trinkets – complain about all those completely impractical knick-knacks right away, before they secure a place in your home (and, worst-case scenario, your partner's heart). If that doesn't do the trick, secretly start throwing things away; make sure you're obvious about it, though.

In your words and actions, make it clear what you think of your partner's sense of order. When you return home from a business trip feeling rested, make sure the first thing you do is complain about the laundry baskets littered about the place. Then start loudly dismantling all the online delivery boxes that have accumulated in your absence. The perfect gift for your partner's birthday? Marie Kondo's *The Life-Changing Magic of Tidying Up*, of course.

If the (former) love of your life comes to you with doubts, it's best not to answer at all. If they refuse to be fobbed off with your silence, remain impassive. When asked things like 'Am I looking old?', whip out this tried-and-tested response: 'Only as old as you are.' When asked, 'What do you think of my new outfit?', a simple 'It's fine' is the best catalyst for conflict, especially when you don't even look up from your smartphone. If a supermodel happens to live on your street and your life partner asks who you think is better-looking, tell the truth.

Gush about how warm, gorgeous, charismatic and successful your neighbour is. Make it clear that your partner could never compete with them. Comment on how other mums and dads do so much more with their kids and 'play a more active role in the marriage' (whatever that's supposed to mean). Drop a casual 'Sometimes I wish you were like X.' Of course, this 'X' should ideally be someone from your mutual friendship circle. Complain about things that categorically cannot be changed. 'You'd be nicer to be around if you were someone else.' That kind of thing.

Disparaging remarks always help to push a marriage closer to the edge. When your partner prepares an elaborate meal, try saying, 'You should really focus on your core competencies.'

Or alternatively, 'I see you've really embraced the "less is more" philosophy with flavour.'

Never admit to your mistakes. Instead, go straight on the counter-offensive, preferably using the word 'but'. When told, 'You're late', respond with 'But at least my hair looks good.' Generally speaking, it's best to treat your relationship like a zero-sum game, where one partner's losses are the other partner's gains. And last but not least: have an affair. If your partner finds out and starts making a scene, be dismissive: 'Come on now, you're just overreacting.' Go on, say it with confidence.

The quiet voice of reason

Your quality of life depends largely on two factors: the quality of your thoughts and the quality of your relationships. We'll come to the quality of your thoughts elsewhere in this book. But in terms of relationships, the quality of your marriage – or other significant romantic partnership – matters most of all. There's no one else you'll spend so much time with during your lifetime, sharing good moments and bad ones too. If your marriage is miserable, your life will be miserable too. No amount of money or status can compensate for that. The research is clear: it's better to be single than to be in a bad relationship.

Two thoughts on this. First of all: there's no such thing as a conflict-free relationship, nor should there be. The very point of marriage is that two brains with a different make-up can solve all manner of problems (everyday life, kids, income, ill health) better than one alone or two that are exactly the same. Minor conflicts are a natural side effect.

Second: when you progress from casual dating to a committed relationship, you're making a conscious choice to work with what you've got. You're deliberately refusing to 'trade up' when something supposedly better comes along. You're investing your energy in the partnership you've already entered – the same way that an entrepreneur invests his energy in his company rather than trading stocks and shares. This pays off in the long term – in both cases. Be loyal or stay single. It's as simple as that.

SEE ALSO **Let Things Fall Apart** (ch. 1); **Have High Expectations** (ch. 5); **Marry the Wrong Person – and Stay with Them** (ch. 41); **Try to Change People** (ch. 44); **Say Everything You Think** (ch. 45)

8

BE A QUITTER

Life is hard. Failure is inevitable, in both the personal and the professional realm. Only crackpots refuse to accept this and choose to push on despite setbacks. Why not cultivate the art of noble quitting instead? Not out of frustration, but as part of a bigger plan. As though that was always your aim. What was it Grandma used to say? 'If at first you don't succeed: try, try again.' Well, I suggest doing the opposite: 'If at first you don't succeed, throw in the towel immediately.' Don't be ashamed of being so defeatist. Life is hard; your despondency is honest and authentic. Oh, and don't wait too long to lay down your arms. Be the first to capitulate. It'll give you a decisive edge in the race for a life of misery.

If something happens to throw you off course, take this as an unequivocal sign to give up at once. Just stay there, lying on the floor. Treat yourself to a generous slice of self-pity – as always, everything is just *so unfair*. Then go out and look for a new purpose. But only stick with the next thing until you hit a roadblock. Even better: quit while you're ahead, so that you'll be on your merry way before you have to experience anything unpleasant.

Better still, spend all your time on pursuits you can't possibly fail at – like checking the weather app on your phone or scrolling through your TikTok feed. Insider tip: if all you do is consume, there's no way you can possibly put a foot wrong. For the first time in the hundreds of thousands of years of human history, it is now possible to exist without failing. It's a golden opportunity. Think about that sense of well-being – yes, rapture – you get when you open the parcel you ordered yesterday with the click of a button! It's the stuff of paradise – like in the Garden of Eden, before they tampered with the apples from the Tree of the Knowledge of Good and Evil.

The quiet voice of reason

One guarantee of an unhappy life is to give up at the first hurdle, or at least the second. I don't know a single person (and I'm sure you don't either) who has never tripped up and fallen flat on their face. This is just down to the topography of life: it's full of potholes that are hard to dodge because they're poorly mapped out. There is a second category of potholes, though: the kind you fall into while expanding your knowledge in your circle of competence. That is to say, no matter what career you're pursuing, you will only be successful in one niche. This is one of the fundamental laws of life. Your circle of competence is where you should truly excel. Efficiency – and with it, your earning power – increases disproportionately to your skills. A supercoder isn't just twice as efficient as an average one, but a thousand times better. The same goes for lawyers, athletes, writers, company founders and investors. Meaning: you should do everything to become an absolute master of your niche. Ideally, you'll become the best – in the world.

When cultivating this mastery, you're bound to tread new ground where there are no more teachers, no more instructions, no more examples to copy. The only way to progress in this uncharted territory is through trial and error. This is the stage where you're going to generate a lot of value, which means you have to persevere. This is what happened to the inventor Thomas Edison: it took him over a thousand attempts to find a model for a light bulb that finally worked. A famous quote from him describes the right mindset: 'I have not failed. I've just found 10,000 ways that won't work.' Persistence pays off. 'Fail fast, fail often' is what they call this tactic in Silicon Valley.

But what if there comes a time when you stop making progress? Maybe even Edison found himself in this situation. I've talked about this with many scientists, including Nobel Prize winners. 'How many attempts before you give up and adopt a completely different approach?' I asked them. The consensus among the brightest minds of our world: the answer isn't set in stone, but the rule of thumb is closer to a thousand than three, more like ten years than three months. So go on: pull yourself up by your bootstraps and try again!

SEE ALSO **Let Things Fall Apart** (ch. 1); **Have High Expectations** (ch. 5); **Only Learn From Your Own Experience** (ch. 14); **Never Be Playful** (ch. 21); **Never Suffer** (ch. 38); **Marry the Wrong Person – and Stay with Them** (ch. 41)

9

BE HYPOCRITICAL

Preaching lofty ideals is all well and good – but don't even think of walking the talk. The perfect formula for a life of misery? *Don't* practise what you preach. Declare, all dreamy-eyed, how important it is to love your partner, but then quietly indulge in the occasional romantic outing while you're away on business. Demand strict compliance – 'Don't mess with my rules!' – but don't be so stupid as to turn down a client's invitation to a (cough) 'conference' in the Caribbean. If you're a CEO, introduce cuts but make sure your bonus remains unscathed. Make a big point of driving to work in an electric car, but then avail yourself of the private jet for your holiday. Loudly campaign for more green tunnels, all the while maintaining a prized fleet of Porsches in the tax haven of Liechtenstein. Lecture your children on the importance of hard work while you spend the day on the garden swing, beer in one hand and phone in the other.

Incidentally, double standards work both ways. You can preach difficult things (like abstaining from alcohol) while simultaneously taking the easy route (drinking as soon as you're alone). This is one of the typical examples. But as a true master of hypocrisy, you must hoodwink the world the other way around: by making the case for more relaxation ('That fitness craze, what a joke!') while secretly exercising strict self-discipline (training for at least an hour a day in your state-of the-art home gym).

Since everyone is a tad hypocritical from time to time, I recommend really pushing the boat out. The greater the chasm between what you say and what you do, the more challenging it will be to hide it from others. But therein lies the appeal! For the ultimate thrill, be a hypocrite on at least a dozen fronts, both in your private life and in business. Eventually your cover will be blown, of course. What if one of your friends points out your double standards? Simply accuse them of not being a real friend. Well, a real friend would never put the truth above friendship!

The quiet voice of reason

All human beings (including me) are hypocritical. It's impossible to be true to our own principles 100 per cent of the time. There are two reasons for this. First of all: principles contradict each other. You'd like to be the perfect family man but have a career at the same time? Unfortunately, you're never going to strike the perfect balance. You want to be in the public eye but also have a private life? Not going to work. You'd like to have an open relationship but also go through thick and thin with one special person? Sorry, not happening. Second: our willpower is only limited. And it fluctuates from one hour to the next.

How far should we allow these double standards to go? An economist would say: to the point where the marginal utility of hypocrisy exceeds the risk of loss of reputation plus the loss of self-respect. Your reputation is gold dust. This alone should force you to keep the hypocrisy to a minimum. The second important term in this formula is self-respect. At what point can you no longer look at yourself in the mirror? Unfortunately, there is no clear line here. The brain is a rationalization machine; it tries to justify every bit of mischief, every reprehensible deed. The author Upton Sinclair writes, 'It is difficult to get a man to understand something, when his salary depends on his not understanding it.' We are infinitely flexible when it comes to justifying our actions, no matter how grotesquely wrong they might be. That's why what we need is a good friend who will look us in the eye and tell us when we are crossing the line beyond commonplace hypocrisy. And most importantly: stop getting riled up at other people's hypocritical ways! Indignation at other people's hypocrisy is the most hypocritical thing of all. Falseness belongs definitively on your not-to-do list.

SEE ALSO **Expect Rationality** (ch. 29); **Consider Money Unimportant** (ch. 32); **Cultivate a Victim Mentality** (ch. 33)

10

CLING TO YOUR BAD HABITS

No one is perfect. So don't you start trying to be! Bad habits are part of your personality. Stand by them. Keep being who you are. If others try to stop you – mostly under the hypocritical pretext of wanting to help – on no account should you back down. These people basically just want to mould you to their own ideals. Don't let yourself become putty in their hands.

Successful people know that the pursuit of a good life involves stamping out character faults. These people spend their younger years honing their strengths and their later years working on their weaknesses. But if you're aiming for a bad life, do neither of these things. Stay true to your toxic emotions, your escapist thoughts, your counterproductive ways. So what if you interrupt every conversation, shower infrequently and swear at the drop of a hat? That's just who you are! Are you arrogant, resentful and careless? That's exactly what defines you!

If you're still trying to find yourself, there's no point looking at your good habits. Your bad habits are where your core personality lies. Good habits are an involuntary by-product of civilization, which means they're completely unnatural. The philosopher Jean-Jacques Rousseau would have said the same thing himself. So don't part ways with your bad habits if they annoy you. For a life of misery, I'd advise staying true to yourself rather than trying to become a better person. Categorically reject any semblance of self-improvement. There are plenty of well-adjusted, modern men and women out there, and not enough pig-headed eccentrics like you!

The quiet voice of reason

Benjamin Franklin, one of the Founding Fathers of the United States of America, was a genius. In fact, he was a genius in more than one area, which is extremely rare. He proved himself to be one of the best statesmen of the eighteenth century, not to mention one of the top scientists of his time. Most of the concepts we associate with electricity – battery, charge, discharge, positive pole, minus pole – come from Franklin. He wrote excellent pamphlets. He was one of America's most successful media entrepreneurs. He invented the lightning rod and bifocals, plus he made significant contributions to fire safety, prevention and insurance in the US. What few people know is that he was anything but satisfied with these outstanding achievements. Instead, he was on a constant quest for self-improvement. At the age of 20, he came up with a plan to 'perfect' his character. He compiled a list of 13 virtues he wanted to cultivate in his life – things like industry, frugality, resoluteness and avoiding unnecessary small talk. He devoted a week to each of these virtues, consciously practising and focusing on them. Then he started the cycle all over again from the beginning.

'Ability may get you to the top,' said the legendary American basketball coach John Wooden, 'it takes character to keep you there.' Now, we can't all be like Franklin or Wooden. But we should at least try to break up with our bad habits.

Since most of us mere mortals find it hard to work simultaneously on our strengths and our weaknesses, my advice is to focus on your strengths while you're still young. You can continue to consolidate these skills when you're past 40, but you're unlikely to start developing new ones after that. Once your strengths – abilities, mindsets, ways of working – are established, concentrate on your weaknesses and set about shedding them. Yes, you'll be in middle age by then, and changing your character takes time, but it's definitely worth the effort.

One way to start is by steering clear of obvious foolishness: no more drinking to excess, no smoking, no self-pity, no moaning, no putting off important tasks, no big promises, no mess and no gossip. Once you get the hang of dodging these pitfalls, you'll find you're already streets ahead of most people.

SEE ALSO **Only Learn from Your Own Experience** (ch. 14); **Get Stuck in Your Career** (ch. 20); **Listen to Your Inner Voice** (ch. 28); **Cultivate a Victim Mentality** (ch. 33); **Try to Change People** (ch. 44)

11

SET THE WRONG GOALS

If you want a dismal life, I recommend setting imbecilic goals for yourself. Try to stay eternally young, for example, or at least look as if you've never aged a day. Make it your goal to turn people's heads when you're walking down the street. Younger people or your peers, either will do. To bring ageing to an almighty halt, haul out the entire arsenal of cutting-edge regimens and treatments at your disposal. Start off nice and gentle with hyaluronic acid, ramp it up to Botox, top it off with a lifting and firming treatment, try laser therapy to stimulate your hair follicles, transform your characterful face with a cute little upturned nose, get a touch of lip filler ... Let the surgeon tamper with your features until you resemble a thousand other women and men who refuse to leave their appearance alone. Become that person without any discerning qualities: make sure anything that's even faintly reminiscent of you, even the tiniest characteristic, is smoothed out once and for all.

Alternatively, pursue goals that are extremely dependent on the role of chance. Aim to become prime minister, a Nobel laureate in literature, or the next Einstein. Do this, and I can guarantee you'll achieve one thing at least: a life of frustration.

If none of the above appeals, then harbour a different kind of nonsensical ambition. Aspire to join the ranks of high-profile celebrities. Do everything in your power to become so famous that strangers take photographs of you wherever you go. Your new-found fame doesn't even have to be based on solid foundations. There are thousands of unfathomably famous people who are only famous for being famous – a media-driven perpetual-motion machine that'll have you caught in a stranglehold and rob you of any privacy.

The quiet voice of reason

For animals, there's no such thing as having an aim in life. Until relatively recently, most people had no reason to agonize about such matters either. Only a few decades ago, everything revolved around survival, a very rational end-goal. This is still the case for many people, like those fighting on the Ukrainian/Russian front, eking out an existence in the slums of Nairobi or hiding among the warring gangs in Haiti.

An entire universe of possibilities opens up when our safety and that of our families is guaranteed. You'd think life would be easier as a result, but unfortunately the opposite is true. The fact is, we're often completely overwhelmed by this freedom. A few thoughts on this below.

Aims in life are fundamentally unjustifiable. They cannot be derived from the laws of nature. Plus, they tend to change as we age. What you thought was worth striving for at the age of 30 will strike you as questionable when you're 60. Why? Because your 60-year-old self has more in common with a 60-year-old you've never met before than the person you were at the age of 30.

As vague as that might sound, aims in life can still be assessed. Some are doomed to fail from the start. For example, if you're concerned with keeping your good looks into old age, you've already lost the battle. You're also bound to lose in the race for everlasting life, no matter how many vitamin supplements you gulp down every day. Aspiring to all-pervasive happiness or fame is also futile. As a social media star, you'll eventually burn out in the global race for attention. Not only is this your own fault, it's also *completely* predictable. 'I don't think I ever wanted to be a banker', I often hear people say. There are some goals and careers (law and acting included) that have a greater potential for dissatisfaction than others. The earlier you recognize what makes you miserable, the better.

Anyway, all this talk of goals and aims in life isn't particularly pleasant. It brings to mind images of goalposts and dartboards. If you miss the target, you get frustrated. But as soon as you hit the target, you find yourself wondering, 'What next?' You have to keep playing the game and scoring more points. Instead of talking about an aim in life, we would do better to talk about having direction. This brings us closer to what the Stoic philosophers understood by 'character', and the heart of the question 'What kind of person would I like to become?' All you need to do is avoid making the mistake of fixating on external goals – beauty, wealth, fame, accolades, renown, popularity – instead of inner development.

So which goals are worth working towards? For over 2,500 years, we have known this much: if you manage to strike toxic emotions like anger, envy, self-pity and irritability from your repertoire, and if you behave rationally and decently, you'll find that happiness and peace of mind come naturally. Bottom line: the direction of travel is more important than speed or any rigidly pursued life goal. Working on your character is the best investment you can make, not to mention the best direction you can take in life.

SEE ALSO **Have High Expectations** (ch. 5); **Be Hyperactive on Social Media** (ch. 15); **Get Rich Quick, Get Smart Quick** (ch. 35); **Never Suffer** (ch. 38)

12

DRINK YOURSELF MISERABLE

Water is for showering. Keep yourself hydrated with alcohol! The odd bottle of wine after a hectic day at work is fine. Maybe even two. Wine – especially strong red wine – is full of antioxidants, which as we all know are good for our cells. Distribute this health benefit throughout the day, preferably starting at noon. Or in the morning, if you like. Begin your day with a sway in your step, maybe with one or two glasses of Prosecco, then slump deservedly into your armchair with something heavier when you get home: vodka for digestion, whisky to wind down, cognac to send you to sleep.

Not everyone truly grasps the benefits of alcohol, so you might have to hide the bottles from your spouse. My tip: for a near-perfect wine-cellar climate, keep them in the garage. Oh, and another thing, always pay with cash; otherwise, your cover will be blown when the next credit-card statement arrives. What about all those empties? Frequent disposal is the only solution. Sadly, a mountain of empty bottles is just as telling as a mountain of full ones.

Despite all your covert operations, it's quite possible that your spouse will chuck you out after a few months of this behaviour. Your kids will want nothing to do with you any more, nor will your friends – who wants to spend all their time around a drunk? You should also bear in mind that you'll repeatedly lose your composure in the office, and you'll end up with the attention span of a toddler. People will gossip behind your back. At some point, everyone will realize what's going on. Then it won't be long before you're unemployed and unable to keep up with the maintenance payments for your ex and the kids.

But never fear; there are always strategies you can explore. Speculate on acrobatic 'investments' in your state of alcohol-induced imbalance. Move to the countryside, where no one knows you. Keep your head above water with odd jobs. Now and then, in your lucid moments, you'll find yourself wondering how you ended up here, how you could do such a thing to your family. Then you'll pull yourself together, go sober for the tenth time – and promptly fall right back off the wagon. The addiction is stronger than you. Everything is stronger than you are now. The physical suffering will mix with your mental distress like gin in your vermouth. There's only one antidote, and that's to up the dose. Soon enough, you'll die from cirrhosis of the liver. There you go – the perfect recipe for a life of misery.

The quiet voice of reason

Between 1.6 and 1.77 million adults in Germany are considered to be dependent on alcohol. In Switzerland, it's between 250,000 and 300,000. That's more than the adult population of Bern and Basel, two of the country's most populous cities, combined. Everyone gets the urge to anaesthetize themselves now and then. Life can be an imposition sometimes. The prospect of blocking out all the difficult crap – the failures, the humiliation, the ups and downs – for a few hours is very tempting. But be careful: self-medicating with alcohol is the first step downhill. I've heard too many stories about promising individuals whose lives have been corroded like acid by booze. The treacherous thing about it is that alcoholism is a slippery slope – no one becomes a drunk overnight. It's more of an inconspicuous sliding motion. What aids and abets this slippery journey is that you don't have to tread darkened pathways to buy the offending substance; you can get it in any supermarket. When I'm out on my grocery run in the morning, I notice unshaven old men placing half a dozen high-proof spirits on the conveyor belt. They have to do it in the early morning (if they're fit to venture out then). There are no reproachful looks. They buy the bottles as if they were croissants. Their addiction is socially accepted.

Put hard drinking towards the top of your not-to-do list. As soon as you catch yourself drinking to numb the pain: stop. No more self-medicating! There are better ways of coping with life.

And don't fool yourself into thinking that a glass of red wine in the evening is good for you. The scientific evidence for this claim is somewhat thin on the ground. If you're bothered about your health, treat yourself to a glass of pomegranate juice instead. It contains even more antioxidants than wine.

SEE ALSO **Feed Your Weaker Self** (ch. 2); **Say Yes to Drugs** (ch. 19); **Get Nihilistic** (ch. 30); **Try to End It All** (ch. 40)

13

GET INVOLVED IN OTHER PEOPLE'S DRAMA

Your neighbours' marriage has been in crisis for years, erupting in varying degrees of hostility at every given opportunity. The quarrelling couple's poor daughter is clearly anorexic and had to be admitted to a clinic. Their son is just 15 years old and has impregnated his teacher, who is 20 years his senior and refuses to get an abortion because she's a devout Catholic. And that's not all there is going on in your neighbourhood. There's that guy on your street whose son failed to show up to his own wedding after falling for his fiancée's sister. Then there's the local fourth-division football trainer, who stole a set of tools complete with nickel-plated screwdrivers from the DIY store – not for the first time, evidently – to do up the clubhouse. Not to mention your kids' recorder teacher, who apparently had to help the caretaker tie his shoelaces – at least that's what she told the children when they stumbled upon the two of them behind the bike sheds.

Oh, the scandal, the drama! Under no circumstances should you stay out of it. Stick your nose in immediately, snoop around everywhere; after all, you have your thoughts about it all, and usually a guilty party in mind too. Try to spark conversation with everyone involved. Let all the sides fill you in on the tiniest details – the truth is often even more dramatic than you'd expect. Try to understand how the different actors think. Suspect only the worst motives.

Act sympathetic, dole out advice to all those involved; that's the only way to get all the juicy details. Quietly scheme a little, all the while posing as a confidant. It'll be even more gripping than Netflix. You'll feel as if you're conducting a high-octane symphony. You'll be right there in the action, living vicariously through their experiences. But while all this is happening, by no means should you actually help – the show must go on, after all! Your job is to coax the maximum drama out of your surroundings, to pass judgement on everyone and everything. Play the role of armchair judge – until the people you're toying with realize who you are: a greedy, miserable little voyeur who sabotages others' lives because you don't have one of your own.

The quiet voice of reason

There are many reasons why we like to get caught up in other people's affairs. First of all, gossip and idle chit-chat provide insights into other people's lives – ideally those that are beyond repair. The spectacle immediately makes our own struggles seem that bit less tragic. Second, scheming and steering fates can be extremely entertaining, providing an escape from the monotony of our own existence. Third, being privy to a drama, be it great or small, makes us feel important. Revealing yourself as an insider can boost your social status, at least in the short term. Finally, there's a fourth (but less common) reason: some of us truly believe that we really can help.

As delicious as it might feel, try to resist. Steer clear of other people's dramas, even if they ask you to get involved. Human dramas are like a vortex that will only drag you down. Because as soon as you're on the inside, you'll lose all ability to be objective. Because over time, your intrigue will downgrade you in your friends' eyes. Because you don't want to damage your relationships with the leading actors; after all, there's a life to be lived once everything has calmed down. Because your time is precious, and you surely have enough on your plate with your own life (if you take it seriously). Because you should respect other people's boundaries. And because you don't want to become a target for their retaliation.

In short: make a point of never interfering in other people's affairs. 'Live and let live' is a sensible motto to keep in mind. If you can't survive without gossip, treat yourself to a trashy magazine every now and again. Delve deep into the plights of royal families without igniting neighbourhood dramas as the price for your curiosity.

But most importantly of all, never give others a reason to meddle in *your* personal life. Set clear boundaries and deal with your own problems behind closed doors. A small cast, three-act play is over faster than an epic opera.

SEE ALSO **Micromanage Your Neighbours** (ch. 18); **Feel Guilty** (ch. 22); **Make Other People Feel Unimportant** (ch. 26)

14

ONLY LEARN FROM YOUR OWN EXPERIENCE

Charlie Munger once said, 'Learn everything you possibly can from your own personal experience, minimizing what you learn vicariously from the good and bad experience of others, living and dead. This prescription is a sure-shot producer of misery and second-rate achievement.'

Munger devoured biographies like others binge Netflix series. Biographies are condensed life lessons. It's bordering on miraculous how so much experience from one person's life can be transported into the reader's mind with just 26 letters, even centuries after the fact. My advice: don't be impressed by this miraculous feat. Why should you concern yourself with the details of other people's lives? Instead, tell yourself every day: 'I'm indescribably unique! No one else's life is anything like mine!' You deserve to treat yourself as the one-off you truly are. Besides, you can confidently ignore our predecessors' accumulated life experiences by pointing out that we're living in a new era now.

Don't just give biographies a miss. Avoid books in general, especially fiction. Novels are simulations of life. They make you stare into the vertiginous abyss from the comfort of your living room armchair, without putting yourself in any danger. But why would you want to do that? Don't you already have enough on your plate with your own problems? Anyway, reading is exhausting. No, there's no need for you to stuff your head with all that nonsense. My advice: stay as uninformed as you possibly can. Be proud of your cultural malnourishment. Your own experience is all that counts.

Ideally, you should even ignore your own past experiences. Stop trying to learn from your mistakes. Good strategies include sugar-coating, pinning the blame on others, denial and forgetting. This is the only way to ensure that disasters keep repeating themselves in your life. And it's the only way to join the ranks of those who make it into the daily news: serial adulterers, people who gamble away their money or keep tripping themselves up with their vanity. Do as they do! In next to no time, you'll find yourself in the worst possible company – and living a sorry excuse for a life.

The quiet voice of reason

Learning from your own mistakes is all well and good, but learning from other people's mistakes is golden. As human beings, we are really rather homogeneous, particularly those of us who inhabit the same cultural milieu. Whether you're British, Swiss, German, Indian, Singaporean, American or Swedish, your life is likely to unfold in a similar pattern, with similar high points and similar concerns. The same is true for the disasters in life. In fact, our daily dramas are quite unoriginal. Self-induced disasters don't come in all that many forms. Which means they are easily circumnavigated – as long as you're aware of them.

This is where biographies come in handy. They're the best object lessons. But beware: not all biographies are created equal. Autobiographies have little to offer in the way of life lessons, as the author is (consciously or unconsciously) concerned with showing the subject in the best light. The same goes for memoirs. They deal with individual episodes from the author's life, but only the ones they want to share, likewise polished to a shine. Biographies written by a third party are the most useful; go for the authorized ones (i.e., still a little idealized) or, better still, unofficial biographies, which are bound to be the most revealing.

When it comes to biographies, the effect of 'selection bias' is another factor to keep in mind. Instead of being presented with a random selection to choose from, what we're given is a skewed sample. Almost all of these books are about successful people, when in fact it would be considerably more helpful to read stories of failed lives. Sadly, no publisher wants to run the financial risk of publishing the biography of a complete nobody. So make sure you change it up often and read novels, too. They are the perfect supplement to biographies. Whatever you do, read as much as you can. As Charlie Munger says, 'In my whole life, I have known no wise people ... who didn't read all the time – none, zero.'

Most importantly, look around. Your environment offers plenty of lessons on the foolish things that are best avoided. I'm not suggesting you delight in them, but you should definitely learn from them. Where exactly did this person go wrong? Why did that relationship break up? Probe like a scientist. More often than not, it's the imbecilic, incidental, silly little mistakes that set a life on a downward path.

SEE ALSO **Get Stuck in Your Career** (ch. 20); **Never Be Playful** (ch. 21); **Get Nihilistic** (ch. 30)

15

BE HYPERACTIVE ON SOCIAL MEDIA

How much time do you spend on social media? Doesn't matter, crank it up a notch. On all platforms. These days, Facebook, Instagram, X, YouTube and LinkedIn aren't enough; you should really be on TikTok and Telegram too. Subscribe to everything, comment on everything, post content like there's no tomorrow! Leave no activity undocumented. The egg you ate for breakfast, your depilatory cream and your opinions on the royal family – they're all equally important.

As well as your genuine profiles, set up a couple of fake accounts where you can really let rip. It's a balm for the soul! Anything goes – the more extreme it is, the more views you'll get: intrigues, lies, plotting, hatred. The great biographer Walter Isaacson wrote, 'There is a truism about internet comment boards: any discussion descends to shouting "Nazi!" within seven responses.' Be that person. Get in there before someone else beats you to it. You don't even have to read the post first; it's not a question of whether the Nazi accusation is founded, it just has to be seen. What matters most is that you are noticed!

Take the business of attention management seriously – the account with all those clicks, likes and love hearts in it should matter to you more than your bank account. Compare yourself every hour with the biggest online stars and influencers. Make it your mission to become one too – by posting even louder, more bizarre content at increasingly short intervals. You'll be amazed at how much you'll gain from this virtual notoriety – specifically, all the time-wasting, brain rot and chronic stress you could ever hope for, not to mention a profoundly sad existence.

The quiet voice of reason

Socrates, Plato, Aristotle, Buddha, Epictetus, Kierkegaard, Wittgenstein, Camus. I'm sure you're familiar with the towering figures of philosophy. I keep asking myself what these great thinkers would have had to say about social media. The answer seems pretty clear to me.

Not one of these philosophers believed that the path of wisdom is to be found by crying out for attention all the time and constantly comparing oneself with others. Quite the opposite. Take any branch of philosophy – Stoicism, Buddhism, Christianity, Enlightenment, analytic philosophy, existentialism, doesn't matter which. All the major schools of thought agree that the path to a good life lies mostly within us. Ego and self-representation are a no-go. For good reasons, backed by research. First of all, comparisons with other people's idealized lifestyles have been shown to lead to depression, dissatisfaction and envy. Well, what else could we expect? People only upload their most flattering images and videos, so it's inevitable that we feel inferior when scrolling. Social media is the perfect envy machine. Second, social media is an attention thief. Our brains get bogged down and overloaded. Our productivity plummets. Third, using a phone while you're talking to someone shows a lack of respect, which the other person will acknowledge with at least an internal 'fuck you'. Fourth, social media cuts you off from real experiences you could have been having while you were busy scrolling. You might have seen it all before, but you've experienced nothing and you've understood even less. There are zero benefits to using social media. Even the few big names who make a living from it now will soon fall from their perches like dead birds. Personally, I've been completely social-media-free for 12 years now, and I've been enjoying the time I've gained as a result.

These days, we all like to shake our heads in disbelief at how people behaved in the past. How could we have deified monarchs? How could we have burned women at the stake for being witches? How could we ever have traded slaves, burned oil, depleted the oceans of fish? How could we keep smoking as if it was the healthiest thing in the world? The history of civilization is steeped in idiocy. Unfortunately, we today are no exception. In a hundred years' time, people will wonder: what on earth was going through these people's minds when they posted and consumed all that inane nonsense? Didn't they have anything better to do with their lives?

SEE ALSO **Trade Your Reputation for Money** (ch. 37); **Say Everything you Think** (ch. 45); **Spin Multiple Plates** (ch. 46); **Fall into the Content Trap** (ch. 52)

16

INDULGE IN ROAD RAGE

In September 2023, I found myself stuck in a traffic jam on the ten-lane I-610 in Houston. We had come to a complete standstill. A shimmering haze hovered above the roofs of the cars. After half an hour, we suddenly started moving. Ten metres' progress, then straight back into the traffic jam. The sandy-brown Nissan Sunny in the neighbouring lane failed to roll forward immediately. Aggressive honking sounded from behind as the woman at the steering wheel frantically tried to start the engine. The ten-metre gap wasn't closing, but the incessant honking of the horn wasn't helping either. Suddenly the driver of the next car got out, gun in hand, and planted himself in front of the Nissan. Pressing the muzzle against the bonnet, he fired three shots through the painted sheet metal, then, seemingly relieved, walked back to his own car and climbed in. No one dared do anything about it. We all just sat there motionless, eyes fixed on the road ahead. A few minutes later, the traffic jam cleared and all the cars moved on. Apart from the Nissan, of course, which by this point had oil dripping from the engine block.

What I experienced that day was an extreme form of road rage. It's a very popular way to vent anger – and to make your life a misery. My advice: always keep a gun in your glove compartment when you're out driving. And if you can't get your hands on a gun, simply chuck a baseball bat in the back. Don't hesitate to whip it out now and again to get the traffic in motion. Someone has to move things along, after all. Pounce at the slightest hint of injustice or negligence on the part of other drivers. But never shoot directly at anyone. I mean, it's not like you're a violent offender. You're just out to provide incentives by punching holes in the odd tyre here and there. And don't worry, there's no need to fear retaliation. No one wants to get dragged into these things, which means you're free to let off steam on the roads to your heart's content. Really, you should feel like a hero: you're acting on behalf of all those scaredy-cats who are waiting virtuously in line, biting their tongues.

Of course, you don't have to go completely apeshit every day like Michael Douglas in the 1993 film *Falling Down*, where he gets into even more of a road rage than our friend from the highway in Texas. Much of the time, a middle finger will suffice. As will driving as close to the car in front as you can – at high speed, of course. And if you're going to overtake, make sure you do it without warning – that's the best way to outmanoeuvre all those slowcoaches. If a car is getting on your nerves, there's nothing to stop you tossing the occasional lighter or plastic bottle out of your window to make them take notice.

And another thing: don't shy away from getting the better of law-abiding citizens. Drive the wrong way down a one-way street to bag the last free parking spot. If other drivers shake their heads at you in indignation when they come away empty-handed, just laugh in their faces. No matter how you choose to provoke, you'll see that rage feeds on itself. The more often you vent your spleen, the less reason you'll need to completely freak out. Go full throttle, do it!

The quiet voice of reason

Have you never sat in traffic seething with rage? Have you never leaned out of the window and sworn at someone? Or honked your horn until it got awkward? I, for one, don't claim to be a saint on the roads. As a driver, I'm one of those people who have more or less weaned themselves off road rage. Age is the main factor at play here. Studies have shown that younger male drivers tend to exhibit more aggressive behaviour on the roads than older male drivers or women. Hot weather also increases the likelihood of a temper tantrum – my experience in sweltering Texas is a case in point. Even so, whenever you get into your car, you should make a conscious decision to leave the anger outside. Set off far too early – that way, you'll never find yourself pressed for time.

If you're stuck in traffic, your frustration is understandable. But let the anger vanish into thin air by acknowledging that you are contributing to this godforsaken tailback just as much as every other driver in it. To do away with the unpleasant feeling that you're wasting a valuable portion of your life in an endless line of cars, make sure you have some audiobooks and good podcasts to hand. By the way, I listen to mine on noise-cancelling headphones instead of the car stereo. It looks a bit eccentric from the outside, but it makes the experience of being stuck in traffic far more enjoyable. One last, ridiculously simple tip: keep a clown's nose in your door compartment. If you're about to become the target of an angry outburst, pop on the red foam hooter and give them a smile. It's disarming.

SEE ALSO **Be Paranoid** (ch. 25); **Cultivate a Victim Mentality** (ch. 33); **Let Your Emotions Define You** (ch. 39); **Celebrate Your Resentment** (ch. 42)

17

SURROUND YOURSELF WITH NEGATIVE PEOPLE

If you're an optimistic sort (caution: not conducive to a life of misery), do yourself a favour and at least hang around with pessimists and killjoys. Before long, they'll succeed in dragging you down into their world of shadows. Happy people will do you no good. At best, their laughter, zest for life and enthusiasm will only fill you with envy. Anyway, doesn't all that insincere positive thinking just drive you up the wall? Positive people are dangerous because they're contagious, worse than the flu. Keep at a safe distance. And forget that stupid saying about how you should always see the glass as half full, never half empty. No matter how full the glass, the truth is that it holds barely anything at all. Quick chemistry lesson required? A water molecule consists of one oxygen atom and two hydrogen atoms, each of which consists of a nucleus and electrons that orbit the nucleus. If you were to stretch a whole atom over an area the size of Paris, the nucleus would be about the size of a melon and the electrons would be loitering somewhere far away in the *banlieues*. Between them? Nada, zilch. Absolutely nothing. So if you think about it, even a full glass is essentially empty.

There's an old saying: 'A negative mind will never give you a positive life.' Take note, dear reader! Well, a life of misery is your express aim, isn't it? Turns out you don't even need to exert yourself to achieve it. The Nobel Prize winner Daniel Kahneman and his colleague Amos Tversky found that negative events have twice the impact of positive ones in our perception. A loss of just 5 per cent on the stock market will trigger as strong an emotional response as a 10 per cent gain. A tooth abscess will cause you as much suffering as a promotion will bring you joy – even though, objectively speaking, the career move is far more important. All you have to do is walk through life with your eyes open: even though positive and negative phenomena are equally distributed by nature, you'll automatically be convinced that the negative outweighs the positive. It follows that a pessimistic attitude is the most natural mindset in the world. You don't need to feel bad about it – actually, yes, go on, please do!

The quiet voice of reason

You are who you hang out with, as they say. If you spend a lot of time with someone who is constantly on a downer, you'll find that their negativity rubs off on you. The term for this is 'emotional contagion'. As with all forms of contagion, we barely notice it creeping up on us. If you surround yourself with negative people, you'll automatically begin to imitate their facial expressions, voice, body language, movements and, of course, their stance – both mental and physical. Before you know it, this negative mindset will become part of your personality. It's a bit like passive smoking. Even if you don't put a cigarette in your mouth, you're still breathing in all that harmful tar, which in turn can entice you to light one yourself. Since this whole process happens unconsciously, my advice to you is to give killjoys and Debbie Downers a wide berth. 'Don't let negative people rent space in your head,' as they say. I've always found this a useful mantra.

There are some companies, cities and regions with a high density of pessimism. If you're often hearing things like 'It's never going to happen anyway' or 'Is that really necessary?', remove yourself from these people.

Why is negativity such a bad thing? One: this kind of mindset is proven to lead to higher stress levels, and chronic stress in turn weakens your immune system. Two: associating with people who are overly negative will hamper your personal development. Your sense of self-worth will take a nosedive, you'll lose confidence. And three: constantly swimming in black bile will simply make you less happy. It's a pretty high price, and for nothing in return.

The good news is this: emotional contagion is a two-way street. Surround yourself with extra-positive people and you'll reap all manner of benefits: a stronger immune system, greater creativity, a more alert mind, contentment, personal growth, more success and a longer life (that's a proven fact).

SEE ALSO **Be Hyperactive on Social Media** (ch. 15); **Make Other People Feel Unimportant** (ch. 26); **Marry the Wrong Person – and Stay with Them** (ch. 41); **Invite Bad People into Your Life** (ch. 48)

18

MICROMANAGE YOUR NEIGHBOURS

Never leave your neighbours in peace – that's the only way to be sure they'll make life hard for you too. Rule of thumb: no compromise, no mercy, no exceptions. Your thoughts should circle your neighbours' property like a sparrowhawk on the prowl. Pay particular attention to potential sources of conflict. Are the boundary lines being respected? Is every tree planted in keeping with the rules, does every weed stop at the border fence? Is next door's car correctly parked in the parking space? Are the quiet hours being observed at night? Do your neighbours have any pets with the potential to cause you an allergic reaction? If so, immediately wave a doctor's report in their faces. Such a pity they'll have to return that cute little puppy after just a few days. Well, they should have asked you before they got it, shouldn't they?

Do your neighbours cook extensively and with wild abandon? If so, they should kindly keep their kitchen windows closed and get an extractor installed. Sure, it might cost them a couple of thousand, but why should you put up with the inconvenience? Don't wait for a flagrant violation; react instantly to the most minor offence. What's that, a few dried-up leaves gathered at the end of your driveway? Get rid of them immediately, please, or else … Forget trying to talk to the neighbours first. To do so would only signal that you're willing to listen to reason. Don't even bother threatening to phone your lawyer; involve them from the get-go. Negotiate a fixed fee for the whole year. That way, you'll have an incentive to use their services as soon as an opportunity arises. React especially strongly and swiftly when new neighbours move in. Lay down the law from day one.

What if your neighbour behaves impeccably, and perhaps even seems friendly and obliging? All the more reason to assume the worst intentions. They're probably just trying to throw you off guard so as to circumvent the BBQ ban. The guiding principle of geopolitics can be directly applied to your neighbourhood relations: peace is just the time between wars. What do you stand to gain from this? That's right – exactly what you were aiming for: a life of misery. Any peace you had will be gone. You'll know you've succeeded when you can no longer even think of your neighbour without your blood pressure shooting through the roof.

The quiet voice of reason

Living alongside other people isn't easy. There are two evolutionary reasons for this. First of all, many species (including human beings) have developed territorial behaviours as a means of protecting their own resources. Even though our modern territories are delimited by plain old fences – and not by stretches of river or fruit bushes any more – these territorial instincts are awakened when we get the slightest suspicion that our boundaries could be breached. Second: like many other species, human beings also form social hierarchies. Neighbours automatically end up competing for social status, be it consciously or unconsciously. It pays to keep both instincts under control. A good neighbourhood is worth its weight in gold.

There's another benefit we know about from criminology: 'collective efficacy'. In 1997, researchers at the University of Chicago discovered that neighbourhoods with higher levels of social cohesion registered lower rates of crime. Why? Because residents are more willing to look out for one another and report suspicious activity when they get along. But money is another factor at play here. Neighbourhoods with a friendly environment are more sought-after, which in turn has an indirect impact on property values.

Not everyone is going to be your cup of tea, and vice versa. We're all only human, and humans aren't perfect, including the ones on your street. But if you're not fond of your neighbours, you don't exactly have to bark it in their faces. Smile at them. Say good morning. Three seconds, that should do. No one expects you to go on holiday together or start a neighbourhood Zen garden project. But a short loan of the power drill? Of course!

SEE ALSO **Be Hypocritical** (ch. 9); **Get Involved in Other People's Drama** (ch. 13); **Say Everything You Think** (ch. 45)

19

SAY YES TO DRUGS

Drugs are a no-brainer. Sure, you could use alcohol to destroy your life, but why take the roundabout route when there are far more efficient substances available? To wind up in a hellscape of drugs without delay, heed my advice. First: tell yourself there's absolutely nothing wrong with trying drugs. Just as you can put this book down whenever you feel like it, you can quit drugs whenever you want. Second: don't just limit yourself to soft drugs (marijuana, mushrooms, sleeping pills); progress to hard drugs (heroin, cocaine, crystal meth, fentanyl) at the earliest opportunity. Life is too short for second-rate junk! Hard drugs are a much faster, more reliable route to dependency. They're also trickier to source, which only adds to the thrill.

Third: you're going to run out of cash pretty fast. When this inevitably happens, simply do what has never failed to ruin millions of other addicts: become a relentless entrepreneur in matters of petty crime. Here, you'll learn skills that will serve you well for the rest of your life. As an added benefit, you'll also get to know a completely new side of society. Write it off as first-hand sociological experience.

You'll lose your job, your family, your home and your reputation, of course. But who wants to lead a straight-edged life? Convince yourself that you'll only keep this up as long as you feel good about it. And feel good about it you will! Like clockwork, your body will let you know what it needs for you to be happy. Give it what it demands before it gets the shakes. And don't even think of seeking professional help. These people are only interested in one thing: spoiling the fun you get from the misery.

The quiet voice of reason

The hackneyed, glaringly obvious advice is: don't even go there. Don't try drugs, not even once. Put them strictly on your not-to-do list. But why be so extra cautious? Because the jump from 'never' to 'just the once' is infinitely bigger than the difference between 'just the once' and 'a thousand times'. It's a bit like murder: whether you kill one person or a thousand, you're a murderer all the same.

Of course you'll come across as a bit strait-laced when you say thanks but no thanks at a drug-fuelled party. But take it as a sign of your strength of character. Withstand the peer pressure; be proud of yourself. Your best bet, really, is to stay away from these parties in the first place. What good could possibly come from going?

Consider the magnitude of this issue: in the USA, there are 100,000 drug-related deaths every year. Picture a graveyard with 100,000 crosses in it. Every cross marks the outcome of a completely foreseeable, agonizing downward spiral. The grave of someone who could have lived a pleasant life. Picture every single one of these corpses at a young age, as a little girl or boy laughing on a swing in the playground. These children, all of them, will be choosing a trip through hell later in life if they cross the line between zero and one. Every year, there's another graveyard with 100,000 graves of people who were once carefree, laughing children.

In case that's not shocking enough for you, remember that drugs destroy not only individual lives but entire cities and nations. For 4,000 years, China was (on par with India) the most powerful empire in the world. Back in 1820, the country generated approximately a third of the global GPD. By around 1950, this share had fallen to just 5 per cent. It was the fastest economic collapse in the entire history of the world. But why did it happen? Drugs were a key factor in China's demise. Great Britain was the world's leading drug trafficker in the nineteenth century. India, a British colony at the time, produced vast quantities of opium. Enticed by the promising market for drugs in China, the United Kingdom took military action and, in two so-called opium wars, forcibly opened up the Chinese empire to the drugs being produced in

India. Even today, the Chinese refer to this time as the 'Century of Humiliation'.

Don't let yourself be humiliated. And if, despite all this, you're still dying to experience 'just the once' how drug-induced hallucinations feel, you could always follow the writer Ian McEwan's advice: 'If you want to know what it's like to take LSD, have breakfast with a four-year-old.'

SEE ALSO **Cling to Your Bad Habits** (ch. 10); **Drink Yourself Miserable** (ch. 12); **Indulge in Road Rage** (ch. 16); **Feel Guilty** (ch. 22)

20

GET STUCK IN YOUR CAREER

Fresh out of university with a BA in hospitality management, Samuel snagged his first job in a travel agency. Pumped full of energy, he got off to a flying start, quickly climbed the career ladder and ended up in the role of assistant branch manager. His clients loved him for his insider knowledge. But before long, the victory march of online booking platforms began and turned the traditional travel agency model upside down. Although the whole industry was eclipsed and became irrelevant, Samuel's loyalty to his job was unwavering. The thought of leaving his familiar office, full of maps and travel brochures, sent shivers down his spine. For a long time, he convinced himself that there would always be a demand for real travel experts – until the day his agency closed its doors for good.

My advice if you want a life devoid of prospects: choose your very first job as your lifelong career. Then stay in the industry for better or worse, even if it's dying. Better to go down with the sinking ship than to update your skills or change sectors.

The quiet voice of reason

Samuel's story shows how our first job often determines our whole career path. Hardly surprising, as career moves are big and fast, especially in the early days of working life. Think of it as a pyramid. Progressing from the base to the next level doesn't require a great deal of luck or any extreme skill. It usually happens automatically, when a space opens up due to natural departures. From the employee's perspective, however, this early progress is a clear sign that they must be on the perfect career path. Let's call this the 'shooting star illusion'. But what happens later? Well, the higher we climb, the thinner the air becomes and the less room there is. At the very top of the pyramid, there's only one CEO position. This isn't such a problem if the sector is growing – if so, it's possible to move roles within the industry. But if the sector is shrinking, it's brutal. Suddenly you feel like you're stuck in a dead-end street. Like our travel expert Samuel.

Maybe the solution would be to correctly predict the rise and fall of various sectors before setting out on a career? Nice idea, but anyone with such impressive clairvoyant abilities wouldn't even need a career ladder; with a couple of savvy investments, they'd become a millionaire. The fact is, no one can predict the exact course that individual professions or industries will take over the next 30 years. Who would have guessed in the 1990s that a lucrative monopolistic newspaper would soon be losing a large portion of its advertising revenue to an unknown start-up with a rather infantile name, Google? Radical innovations, by their very definition, are unpredictable. If they weren't, we would already know about them today.

There's only one way to avoid getting stuck in dead ends, and it's to become a learning machine! All the successful people I know suck up new, relevant knowledge like sponges. That's their secret. Charlie Munger once said, 'I constantly see people rise in life who are not the smartest, sometimes not even the most diligent, but they are learning machines. They go to bed every night a little wiser than they were when they got up and boy does that help, particularly when you have a long run ahead of you.' Learning is even more important than intelligence. In a commencement speech at the University of California, Munger warned graduates, 'You are hooked for lifetime learning. And without lifetime learning, you people are not going to do very well. You are not going to get very far in life based on what you already know. You're going to advance in life by what you learn after you leave here.'

Bottom line: don't fall prey to the 'shooting star illusion'. The fact that your career is taking off in the early stages isn't a reliable indicator that you'll be flying high for the next 20 years. My advice for when you're starting out: try your hand at different lines of work, don't get fixated on just one sector. Once you've established yourself in one industry, you should keep deepening and expanding the knowledge you possess in your circle of competence. There's always the chance of knowledge and skills becoming obsolete. It won't happen overnight, but it might over a period of just a few years. Read avidly. Fifty books a year. Ten long articles per week. Be paranoid about your knowledge and your abilities; they rarely reach as far and wide as you would think. If your profession is becoming irrelevant, make sure you get out early – before the ship starts to sink.

SEE ALSO **Be Unreliable** (ch. 3); **Be a Quitter** (ch. 8); **Only Learn from Your Own Experience** (ch. 14); **Go Where the Competition is Strong** (ch. 49)

21

NEVER BE PLAYFUL

Are you familiar with *American Gothic*, the 1930 painting by American artist Grant Wood (1891–1942)? It's one of the most parodied paintings ever. In it, a farmer and his daughter, who looks more like his wife at first glance, are standing side by side. The man is holding a pitchfork. There's a farmhouse with a neo-Gothic gabled window in the background. Father and daughter stare out into the world, all sombre and serious. You must have seen this painting before, at least the odd cartoon version – for me, it is *the* most iconic representation of austerity. If you want to really make your life miserable, this is exactly how to go about it – be sullen, sombre, uptight, joyless. Suppress those playful impulses. Never indulge in any kind of frivolity. Even a touch of informality is taboo. Follow this advice and you'll find yourself in good company. If you read the Bible, you'll conclude that even God can't take a joke. The

Success Through Less

Nobel Prize for Physics winner Richard Feynman was an exuberant individual who played the bongos in his free time and didn't take life even the slightest bit seriously. The American mathematician Claude Shannon, known as the 'Father of the Information Age', rode a unicycle while simultaneously juggling. Leonardo da Vinci's notebooks are full of playful sketches and fanciful ideas. Be wary of this kind of amusement! If you emulate these great figures, your dream of a miserable life will never become a reality. In the worst-case scenario, you might even playfully stumble into some kind of success.

My first publisher, Daniel Keel, the founder of Diogenes publishing house in Switzerland, was a joker. One time when I was visiting him, he stretched his arms out and said, laughing heartily, 'The left hand is birth, the right hand is death, and between them are all the silly things in life.' To be sure of a terrible existence, stay true to the opposite sentiment: 'The left hand is birth, the right hand is death, and between them is nothing but the grim, serious reality of life.' Complain incessantly about your life – not just because it's hard, but as a matter of principle. Live by the motto of puritanism, accurately described by the philosopher and psychotherapist Paul Watzlawick in his 1983 book *The Situation is Hopeless, But Not Serious*: 'You may do anything you want, as long as you don't enjoy it.'

The quiet voice of reason

At the age of 18, I decided not to crack a smile for a year. I was convinced that laughing drained all my energy because it required moving your facial muscles. I told myself it was better to save my energy for thinking, where it could be used to solve the problems of the world. So from that point on, I ceased to smile and even made a point of avoiding my witty contemporaries. I kept up this nonsense for exactly a year, with nothing to show for it at the end. I hadn't even solved *one* of the world's problems. I felt exactly how I looked: downright miserable. Then I put a stop to the idiotic experiment and began to move the corners of my mouth, even letting them curl upwards. Lo and behold, girls started chatting to me again, life became brighter and more interesting. I'm hardly a joker these days, but I've definitely developed a lighter side, and it has clearly done me good.

As irritating as life can be sometimes, there are only good things to be gained from adopting a playful approach. According to René Proyer, a psychologist at the Martin Luther University Halle-Wittenberg in Germany, playfulness promotes creativity. A Canadian study has also shown that it makes us likeable and reduces stress. Funny people are happier – that much is clear. So here's a little tip for more joviality in life: compile a personal 'dopamine list'. These are activities you can do from time to time in order to jolt you out of the daily grind and make you feel exhilarated. My own list contains things as simple as listening to jazz, aimlessly cruising around the city on my e-bike, playing on a flight simulator, roughhousing with the kids and watching stand-up comedy on YouTube. Another good idea is to laugh at your misfortunes. You'll have ample opportunity.

As a serious, self-controlled human being, it isn't easy to pull playful threads from the fabric of your psyche. Give it a try anyway; it doesn't cost a penny. Life is hard, but at the end of the day it's also a game. Levity is what sets the best thinkers, athletes and artists apart. As the great novelist and playwright Christopher Isherwood said: 'Only those capable of silliness can be called truly intelligent.' Anyway, no one will be talking about you a hundred years from now, so it's neither here nor there if you adopt a slightly more playful approach to life, starting today.

SEE ALSO **Indulge in Road Rage** (ch. 16); **Get Nihilistic** (ch. 30); **Catastrophize** (ch. 31)

22

FEEL GUILTY

For a life without hope, I recommend feeling perpetually guilty. It's easy; never before have there been so many things you can do wrong. We are living in a veritable supermarket of sins. There's a whole array on offer – just take your pick! You'll find a particularly extensive range on the shelf labelled 'Personal Conduct'. Give yourself a hard time about the chips you ordered today. And those vegetables you failed to cook. Oh, and you haven't done any sport today? Tut, tut.

For guilt by the bucketload, head straight to the 'Interpersonal Relations' section. Fill your trolley with a healthy measure of guilty conscience for all those little white lies that have crept into your everyday life. And when it comes to interpersonal resentments, please, always instantly point the finger at yourself.

The shelf marked 'Close Relationships' is where you'll find guilt for all kinds of role-related conflicts. As a man, you should be affectionate, funny, confident, passionate, spontaneous and, at the same time, a bastion of calm – a blend of the Dalai Lama, Roger Federer, James Bond and Ernest Hemingway. Can't quite manage that? Shame on you! As a woman, it goes without saying that your duty is to be the answer to any man's dreams. Be beautiful, clever, athletic, warm-hearted, the organizational whizz of the family and (from time to time) the best lover your partner has ever had. Not always in the mood to bake, draw or play football with the kids? Perhaps you have a particularly good rapport with one of your offspring? Is it possible that you love that one child a little bit more than the others? Aha, there we go! If you're not feeling guilty yet, your distinct lack of conscience should at least prompt pangs of guilt.

Now head over to the 'Social Responsibility' section, where you're sure to hit paydirt. That's right: there's so much more you could be doing for your neighbourhood. For example, you could organize a street party once in a while, like your neighbours do every year. Right next to that is the 'Environment' section. Do you own a car? Are you flying abroad for your holiday? Do you buy meat in plastic packaging? Do you eat meat at all? Salad in winter? Oranges in summer? You'll find XXL packs of guilt in this department, but absolutely no mercy. The fact that you exist, that you're missing your personal net-zero target with all the carbon dioxide you exhale, that you emit methane every time you fart must have you wanting the ground to open up and swallow you. Go on, throw in another half a kilo of original sin – you know, the stuff God planted in your cradle but you keep forgetting about because it's somewhat illogical.

Checked off all the items on your shopping list yet? Great, all you need before you head to the checkout is some collective guilt. Think about Auschwitz, the slave trade, witch burnings and all the other crimes your predecessors perpetrated. My general recommendation for a truly wretched existence: feel responsible for the state of the world in general!

The quiet voice of reason

We get caught up in conflicts from an early age. The older we get, the more we do and experience, the more closely woven the fabric of these conflicts becomes. Maybe you're holding out hope that the tangled web will eventually come undone? That the people you've disappointed, betrayed, lied to or pushed aside will forgive you? That they'll throw their arms around you and everything will be okay again? Unfortunately, that's just not how it works.

'One of the most terrible and deceptive words in the English language is "closure", says the British author Ian McEwan. 'In movies and novels you get closure sometimes, but in life it rarely happens, if at all.' We never completely wrap up the things we go through in life. The scars remain, we carry them with us. Face it: life will never be neat and tidy again. It was the purest it was ever going to be on the day you were born.

Success Through Less

Look to Nobel Prize winner Richard Feynman and mathematician John von Neumann if you want to radically evade the daily offers in the local guilt supermarket. Feynman once said, 'Von Neumann gave me an interesting idea: that you don't have to be responsible for the world that you're in. So I have developed a very powerful sense of social irresponsibility as a result of von Neumann's advice. It's made me a very happy man ever since.' Social irresponsibility – think that sounds conceited? Well, it would be positively megalomaniacal to take on the whole world's guilt. Apparently someone did this in the past; his name was Jesus. Know your place: stop wallowing in your bath of guilt and get on with it.

SEE ALSO **Live in the Past** (ch. 27); **Cultivate a Victim Mentality** (ch. 33); **Celebrate Your Resentment** (ch. 42)

23

PRACTISE INGRATITUDE

The Zurich to London flight was delayed. First by 20 minutes, then by 40. Murmurs rippled through the overcrowded terminal. The guy sitting next to me at the departure gate was clearly having difficulties emotionally processing the delay. 'Oh, come on!' he cried. 'This is outrageous!' We finally boarded, but then came the announcement: 'We're sorry, but take-off will be delayed by 30 minutes due to heavy outbound traffic. We apologize for the inconvenience.' While most of us barely reacted, unfastening our seat belts at most, my gate neighbour finally snapped. What a load of bullshit; he'd never be flying with Swiss again! This place was a torture chamber! He was gesturing so wildly that even the people in the back row were craning their necks to watch. The flight attendant had to go over and personally reassure him.

I viewed him as an interesting specimen to be studied. This man,

I thought, has the perfect mindset for a sorry life. There he was, sitting in a feat of technology that could transport him from Zurich to London, and all of this from the comfort of his own seat! Just a few generations ago, the journey would have taken over a month: an ordeal to be endured on foot in holey shoes, without maps or waterproofs, wearing the same sweat-soaked underwear, sleeping in bug-infested beds overnight, with highwaymen lurking at the side of the road, and ending with a crossing to Dover on stormy seas.

If you're keen to lead a crappy life, take a leaf out of this man's book. Get worked up about everything that doesn't run completely smoothly, and remain intolerable until you have achieved a paradisiacal degree of comfort. If someone gives you a gift you don't like, let them know. There are so many other, more fitting gifts they could have chosen, you're only telling the truth. Be ungrateful that you were born in this country, in this century and not when the universe in all its vast glory was prepared for your arrival. Ingratitude is essential for a terrible life. Ideally, you should be ungrateful that you're even on the planet. Yes, you might be healthy and intelligent, but rather maddeningly, you don't look like George Clooney or Charlize Theron. Focus on everything that's going wrong – there's no use talking about what's working for you.

The quiet voice of reason

When you're out on a bike ride, you instantly feel the headwind but barely notice the tailwind. The American psychologist Tom

Gilovich and Shai Davidai discussed this 'headwinds/tailwinds asymmetry' in 2016 in the *Journal of Personality and Social Psychology*. The phenomenon is not unique to bike rides; it applies to many aspects of life. The difficulties we face – the hurdles and stumbling blocks we encounter – are far more apparent to us than all the things in life that run smoothly. We get riled up about the bothersome individuals who are always standing in our way. The spilt milk that could be avoided with better-designed packaging. Our friends' shortcomings. The endless litany of software updates on our computers. The forms we have to fill out for an insurance quote. And, of course, when the train is delayed.

At the same time, we ignore the tailwinds in life, even though they are much stronger. Think about it: unless you happen to be one of the very youngest readers of this book, you have already far exceeded the historic natural life expectancy of human beings. Remember that you have access to an infinite treasure trove of knowledge and nuggets of wisdom – and that the price of a good book is nothing compared to the benefits to be derived from it. Think about how you live in a country where you can freely express your opinions. Your ancestors fought for this without you ever having to pay for it.

Every day on my bike ride to the office – sometimes with a tailwind, sometimes with a headwind – I cross the Kirchenfeldbrücke in Bern. How much does it cost me to cross this bridge? Not a cent! I don't have to assemble a single iron girder myself. A previous generation did the hard work for me.

The bicycle was perfected over centuries, but we don't owe anyone a licence fee to own or ride one. A good 99 per cent of the things we use – from pencils and coffee machines to the alphabet – work seamlessly. This is even true of our bodies: in the time it takes you to read this sentence, your immune system will have eliminated billions of harmful viruses and bacteria. Indefatigably and for no charge. Generally speaking, most of the things in life are given to us for free – the landscape, sunlight, the warmth on our skin and, most importantly, the ability to experience all of these things. The next time your plane is endlessly circling, in a queue, and you're waiting impatiently to land – from your chair in the sky! – just remember the tailwind.

SEE ALSO **Surround Yourself with Negative People** (ch. 17); **Never Be Playful** (ch. 21); **Get Nihilistic** (ch. 30); **Catastrophize** (ch. 31)

24

TRUST YOUR BANKER

If a dismal life is your destination of choice, allow obscure incentives to be your guide. Study at institutions that value and reward rote learning over comprehension. If you're a journalist, write for media outlets that generate revenue by reach instead of charging customers directly. You'll prize scandalous headlines over objective reporting. If you're a banker, encourage customers to trade on the stock market as often as possible. It'll be a nice little earner for the bank – with money taken straight from your customers' pockets. If you're a doctor, recommend complicated but completely unnecessary surgery – a handy way to boost your income. Wherever an incentive beckons, nod eagerly and say yes to an ultimately unpleasant life.

The quiet voice of reason

If you can't quite work someone out, don't immediately go poking around in their childhood, analysing their family conflicts or doubting their intelligence. Start by looking at what motivates them, i.e. the incentive system in which they operate. Around 90 per cent of human behaviour can be explained by incentives. Charlie Munger wrote, 'Show me the incentive and I will show you the outcome.' Most people react instantly and consistently to strong incentives, even ones that are ethically questionable or completely nonsensical. This is what's known as the 'incentive super-response tendency'. The logical but tragic result: idiotic incentives lead to idiotic behaviour.

Two things to consider here. First, don't let yourself be a person who initiates stupid incentives. Second, don't fall victim to idiotic incentives. Let's start with the first point. As a lawyer, you're concerned with client satisfaction. As a health-care professional, you care about your patients' health. As an adviser, you're invested in your customers' outcomes. But at the end of the day, your own income is paramount. You therefore have an inbuilt incentive to bill for as many hours as possible – far more than necessary. In all three professions, you're caught in a questionable incentive system; if you seek primarily to benefit yourself, you'll automatically cause your clients, patients or customers financial damage and compromise a long-term relationship of trust. If your client gets suspicious that you (their lawyer) are billing them for too many hours, the trust will be gone. And not just their trust in you as an upstanding citizen. Even worse, their trust in your professional competence will also be obliterated thanks to the 'halo effect'. You'll lose money, and your reputation will suffer.

Another example: salespeople usually receive commission for the sales volumes they generate. This in itself isn't particularly problematic. But it does become counterproductive when billing happens quarterly and a higher percentage commission is applied from a certain sales threshold. This leads to what is known as 'channel stuffing', where the salesperson crams all the annual turnover into a single quarter and doesn't give two hoots about the rest of the year.

Academia also operates according to a rather murky reward system. If you're an academic, your career is largely determined by the number of articles you publish, which journals you're published in and how often these articles are cited. What you really want is to be a brilliant researcher, but you find yourself following a similar logic to the most imbecilic of YouTube or TikTok stars. Rather than investing in valuable research, you're spending a good chunk of your time on mindless publishing. Before you decide to embark on a career in research, you should get clued up about how academic life works. Sadly, the days when Albert Einstein and Niels Bohr used to document their research in well-written letters are over.

Moving on to the second point: don't fall prey to idiotic incentives. Your banker has an incentive to sell the greatest possible number of financial products for the most exorbitant management fee possible. They will encourage you to trade on the stock market as often as you can, because each transaction generates fees. This is all well and good for the bank and the banker – but it's bad for you. So: never trust your banker. Not because they are a bad person. Simply because their incentive system is at odds with your best interests.

If you become alert to the dangers of ill-advised incentive systems, you'll experience the world in a completely different way. Just as a chemist views everything from a molecular perspective, you'll start to see humanity's actions from an incentive perspective. 'Don't ask your barber if you need a haircut,' as they say. Keep this in mind. Not only will it protect you from adventurous hairdressers, it'll also stop you subscribing to phoney incentive systems.

SEE ALSO **Consider Money Unimportant** (ch. 32); **Get Rich Quick, Get Smart Quick** (ch. 35); **Trade Your Reputation for Money** (ch. 37); **Go Where the Competition is Strong** (ch. 49)

25

BE PARANOID

Everyone is following you. Everyone wants to trip you up. The whole world has conspired against you. Bask in these cheery thoughts. You'll see critical glances everywhere you look, hear whispering voices wherever you turn. If something bad happens to you, take it as undeniable proof that your whole environment has one sole aim: your demise, your ruin, your downfall. Racked with stress and fear, you'll be incapable of achieving anything productive. You can forget about your career. Creativity? Kiss that goodbye. Playfulness? That would only be your undoing. People will probably say you're paranoid. But the truth is, you're just being vigilant. Friendships? They're only ever fleeting. Someone's being nice to you? Stay on guard: they definitely want something from you. Unlike your former friends, who see the world through rose-tinted glasses, you'll see that person exactly for who they are:

a beast that's bound to attack at the first opportunity.

Warren Buffett owns one of the biggest conglomerates in the world, with almost 400,000 employees, but the headquarters is manned by just 24 people, including his PA. For him, the ideal kind of management culture is a 'seamless web of deserved trust' – an approach that saves on bureaucracy, monitoring and controlling. You, on the other hand, needn't be so naïve. You know there's no such thing as 100 per cent trust; not even 10 per cent trust. If you're a manager, you have a simple choice to make: micromanagement or your own inevitable downfall. The same applies to your private life: your marriage contract should be at least 50 pages long, otherwise it's best not to tie the knot. Oh, and never let your kids out of the house without a tracking device (AirTag, Apple Watch, etc.).

Trust is bronze, prudence is silver, but mistrust is gold. Sure, this mindset will strip you of any playfulness or zest for life, but it's the only way to keep your grip on reality. Should a pleasant breeze ever waft through your life, completely out of the blue, trust it at your peril. Behind that breeze, a storm is brewing.

The quiet voice of reason

Mistrust is only rational in unfamiliar situations. Say your banker recommends a new 'structured product' that just so happens to have a high management fee. Or you receive an email from an African king who wants to bequeath his inheritance to you. Scepticism is the only sensible response here. Wariness is also advisable in cases where someone supplies contradictory information. When facts and stories don't add up. When something sounds too good to be true. When someone pressures you to make a quick decision, especially if there's money involved. And when someone you know well suddenly changes their behaviour for no apparent reason. In short, a healthy dose of suspicion will protect you from potential stumbling blocks.

That said, there are two instances in which mistrust is counterproductive. First, when it fails to turn to trust after several years of smooth cooperation. If you think you still have to read your spouse's emails after ten faultless years of marriage, then something is definitely amiss. Second, when mistrust morphs into paranoia. We're talking extreme, irrational beliefs that have no bearing whatsoever on reality. For example, if you're convinced that your neighbour bugged your garden years ago, even though this suspicion is completely unfounded. It's true that we all have irrational thoughts *sometimes*. The problem arises when these kinds of delusions occur *often*. Paranoia kills your zest for life, your relationships and, not least, your efficiency, because it monopolizes a huge amount of your brain's capacity. So, add paranoia to your not-to-do list.

What can you do to combat this extreme form of mistrust? One answer is to look at things objectively, perhaps with the help of a friend. Where exactly is this evidence of the world conspiring against you? Take a piece of paper and write down your observations. I guarantee you this: if you stick to the facts, the sheet will remain blank. Another thing you can do is assume that you're not as important as you think. People have other things to do than go around setting traps for you all the time. Last of all: if reason alone isn't enough to convince you not to be paranoid, take some medication to calm you down. It exists, and it works. You can get it from your GP – and no, you're not your doctor's guinea pig.

SEE ALSO **Have High Expectations** (ch. 5); **Catastrophize** (ch. 31); **Ruminate** (ch. 36)

26

MAKE OTHER PEOPLE FEEL UNIMPORTANT

What's the point in taking an interest in other people? Save yourself the effort. Don't even try to act like you care about their joys and sorrows. If you really must listen, do so passively. Quietly let other people know what you think of them, i.e., nothing at all. Oh, and never bother to learn their names. The only name you need to know is your own; proclaim it loudly to the world at every available opportunity. Remembering these things is an absolute waste of your intellectual capacity. Politicians might have to do it, but why should you? The person you're talking to could just as well have been baptized with a different name – it's all completely arbitrary, you see. It's enough that you're giving them the time of day, whatever their name might be.

If someone comes up to you with a tale of woe, simply brush their concerns aside. Tell them, 'It's not that bad!', 'It'll be fine!'

or 'Don't overreact!' You can also let a little smile creep onto your face; that way, they'll get the message that they're being over the top. Put their problems into perspective. Tell them, 'This kind of thing happens all the time to people all over the world.' It's the absolute truth.

Not taking other people seriously is an effective emotional firewall. Empathy would only riddle this wall with holes. Suddenly you'd be flooded with their feelings, like foreign passengers aboard your journey through life. Anyway, it's not like anyone has paid you to make others feel important, is it? So you don't have to do it. There are plenty of psychologists who charge extortionate hourly rates for that sort of thing.

For a miserable existence, I recommend ignoring not only other people's feelings, but also their opinions, ideas and ways of thinking. Imagine what would happen if someone other than you was ever right. You'd be forced to reconsider your position! And you're definitely not going to do that, because like every connoisseur of the miserable life, you know that the world revolves around you. Everyone else is insignificant. You can always feign a little interest in others if really necessary. Ask them what they ate for breakfast, for example. Or ask them their name a dozen times but instantly forget it every time. All the feigned interest you could ever need.

The quiet voice of reason

The 7 Habits of Highly Effective People by the American author Stephen R. Covey is a classic book on personal development. One of Covey's seven rules is 'Seek first to understand, then to be understood.' Normal listening isn't enough when it comes to understanding. You have to take it up a notch. Covey calls this 'empathic listening'. It's about genuinely trying to grasp the other person's thoughts and empathize with their emotions. Most people only hear part of the conversation, i.e., the part they want to hear. But empathic listening requires us to fully engage with the other person. No phone on the table, no getting distracted, no pre-formed judgements.

The advantages of empathic listening are obvious. One: you establish trust with your interlocutor, which means they'll be more open to hearing your point of view when the time comes. Two: when you listen attentively, there's no need to make assumptions about the other person's motives. If you give them time to talk, their motivations will naturally come to light. Three (this one's actually pretty hackneyed): a problem is easier to solve when approached from different perspectives.

Now, empathic listening isn't everyone's bag. Most of us communicate the important things between the lines, so it takes a little bit of life experience to know not to take what people say literally. Another tip: try not to get too emotional, or you won't be able to listen objectively any more.

In recent decades psychologists have been exploring 'active listening'. It turns out that people can largely train themselves to do this – just as we can learn to listen to music or understand art. Ultimately, all of this can be summed up using the simple '3C life rule' developed by the popular former Swiss president Adolf Ogi: 'Carefully Cultivate Connections'.

SEE ALSO **Be an Asshole** (ch. 4); **Be Hypocritical** (ch. 9); **Surround Yourself with Negative People** (ch. 17)

27

LIVE IN THE PAST

Danny, now in his late fifties, is a former second-division footballer who led his team to countless victories in his twenties. In his home town, his name is synonymous with sporting excellence. Danny never felt more alive or more important than in those years. Though his life took unexpected turns as he got older, he has never truly left the glory days behind him. His house is like a shrine to the past, bedecked with trophies, photographs and newspaper cuttings from his time as a pro footballer. When he meets up with old friends – some of whom jokingly call him 'Maradanny' in a nod to the legendary Argentine dribble artist Diego Maradona – the conversation always revolves around that bygone era. Ten years ago, Danny was invited to coach the local under-14 team. It would have been an opportunity to relive his passion for football, but he turned it down. Coaching kids would have been beneath dannyhim, and would have tarnished his memories. Danny has made himself so comfortable in his own past and lives so deeply immersed in it that he has not the slightest interest in stepping out into the here and now.

If you want to miss out on all that life has to offer, be like Danny and live in the past. That way, you'll always know exactly how everything feels. You'll simply keep replaying the same infinite loop as you luxuriate in the glorious days of old. Or, if you prefer things a little darker, why not relive your former disasters? Mourn past love affairs, lost jobs and time with your young children. The past will take over and you'll have barely any time for the present. You'll be stuck in the cured concrete of your own history.

The quiet voice of reason

How much of your life should you devote to the past? The bare minimum. Using the past as a resource, however, learning lessons from it and letting go of unrealistic expectations, will help you make it through the present in one piece. Not only that, it will also guide you successfully into the future. The best strategy is to write these lessons down in a notebook that you return to now and then. In this way, you can bury the past in good conscience. Replaying the dark periods of your life over and over will only make you feel even darker. As for the good times? Well, it's like listening to your favourite music: it feels good to hear those songs, of course it does, but listening alone isn't going to change your life.

None of the successful people I know are nostalgic. They use very little mental energy thinking about days gone by. As soon as they have learned lessons from the past – when there is nothing left that could still be of use to them in their present – they turn their attention to the future.

Devotees of Stoicism, a school of philosophy that originated around 2,000 years ago, had a similar view: there are some things we can change, but other things are beyond our reach. The past definitely belongs in the latter category. Just accept it. There's no point wishing things were different. And don't make a meal of it; if you go to the psychotherapist for five years to 'come to terms' with your past, you're definitely doing something wrong.

Sadly, this is something we clearly struggle to do, even collectively. Whole nations get bogged down in their history. Many heads of state harp on about their country's (non-existent) glorious past to instil a sense of national identity in their people and legitimize their power. This is dangerous, because it leads to historical misrepresentation, revanchism and idiotic decisions (i.e. Russia), whereas countries that have no origin myth (Taiwan) or have largely debunked such myths (Switzerland) are freer and act more rationally.

My first job after university was at Swissair. How proud I was to see 'our' planes at the airports of the world. When the airline went bankrupt in 2001, I spent months mourning that golden era. Until a former Swissair colleague gave me a dressing-down and said to my face, 'That's enough. Focus on the future – that's where life happens!' Whenever I catch myself mourning the past, I stick to the following rule: 30 seconds, not a moment more! I've trained myself to have an almost allergic reaction to my private nostalgia.

SEE ALSO **Get Stuck in Your Career** (ch. 20); **Ruminate** (ch. 36); **Celebrate Your Resentment** (ch. 42)

28

LISTEN TO YOUR INNER VOICE

Trying to find yourself? Need some direction? The solution is very simple: listen to yourself. There, deep within your brain, lies the secret to your identity – your inner voice. Can't decide what to do with your time, your life, your relationships, your career? No problem. Your inner voice will tell you. Always trust that voice. It will be delighted to accommodate your request for advice and inspiration. It will fill every little gap in your mind – with anxieties, fears, desires, warnings, flash-backs and to-dos, with soundbites you've picked up, embarrassing episodes from your youth, things that have happened and other things you've merely imagined. Your inner voice will supply all of this, often unprompted. Nice and varied like a YouTube playlist, always carefully addressing your latest fleeting interests and needs. Because your inner voice, so they say, is your compass. Your compass for a life of misery.

To lead a truly dreadful existence, you should embark on about a hundred tasks and never really finish any of them. Your inner voice will help you to achieve exactly this. It will jump from one subject to the next, then back again. It will demand one thing one second and the opposite the next. Your life will frantically zigzag all over the place, with no direction or purpose. Most importantly, you'll never be bored again – your inner voice is perfectly capable of prattling on and on for 24 hours a day, 7 days a week. Listen to it carefully, don't ever question what it says. After all, anyone who can talk like that must be extremely knowledgeable!

The quiet voice of reason

Apparently, human beings have 100,000 thoughts per day. That's about two every second, not counting the time we spend sleeping. It's a plausible figure, one quickly confirmed by a short spell of self-observation. Very few of these thoughts are intentional. Very few are original. Even fewer are relevant. Collectively, this jumble of mental musings can be referred to as our 'inner voice' – a volcano incessantly spewing forth hot fragments of thought that immediately turn cold. It's almost criminally idiotic to expect any guidance from this chaos. A few reflections on this below.

One: you are not your inner voice; you are merely its audience. It's up to you to decide whether you want to listen. Since your inner voice is mostly a signal jammer, I recommend ignoring it if possible. Banish it to your not-to-do list. Your inner voice is insatiable. It is forever reporting errors, sounding alarms, reminding you of something that absolutely mustn't happen or something you should be forgetting. Your inner voice plays out a non-stop melodrama.

Two: unfortunately, there's no way to switch off your inner voice. That is, unless (unlike me) you're someone who's able to meditate and block out all your thoughts. But even if you *do* happen to be a better meditator than me, it's not like it's possible to remain in this state 24 hours a day. As soon as the calm of the (successful) meditation has passed, the cacophony will start up again. There has to be a different way of dealing with this babble of voices. Here's one solution: jot down the few relevant messages from your brain on a piece of paper, a calendar or a to-do list. Make a point of doing this regularly. For example, my iPhone is programmed so that when I press the side button, I can record a voice note, which is instantly converted into a note on my to-do list. I don't have to open an app or start typing; I don't even have to turn off the hob or stop brushing my teeth. Over time, the babble of voices dies down because I know that the important thoughts have been filed away and I no longer have to lug them around in my brain. I go through my to-do list twice a week and turn the notes into calendar entries, assign deadlines to them. I also – and this is very important – delete anything that turns out to be unimportant when I think about it in greater detail. Goodbye, brain traffic. Goodbye, endlessly repeating thought loops.

Three: your inner voice has astonishingly little bearing on reality. Most of the time, it's our thoughts that cause us stress, not reality itself. Stay firmly in the outside world. Tackle the real problems. Focus on your long-term goals and the tasks on your agenda today. This will give you clear direction.

Four: even when it comes to direction in the wider sense – i.e., the question of what you want to do with your life – you should deliberately ignore your inner voice. Look at your concrete skills instead. What are your proven strong points? Focus on them. Let's say you're standing in the shower and you hear your inner voice shout, in a rush of excitement, 'Be a singer!' but you're actually much better at maths than music – become an accountant, auditor or statistician. The world needs more number whizzes. Terrible singers, it can do without.

SEE ALSO **Be Unreliable** (ch. 3); **Be a Quitter** (ch. 8); **Live in the Past** (ch. 27); **Let Your Emotions Define You** (ch. 39)

29

EXPECT RATIONALITY

If you love talking to brick walls or banging your head against them, be confident that your fellow humans are all rational beings. Use crystal-clear arguments to try to get your partner, your colleagues, your boss, your customers or your neighbours on side. It won't be long before you're losing your mind.

Have you invested money on the stock exchange? Trust that other investors behave as rationally as you, and that the stock market is an accurate reflection of a company's true value. It's only logical, isn't it? By adopting this approach, you freely accept that you'll miss out on all the great deals – for example, the next time panic breaks out on the stock markets. You'll also only recognize bubbles once they have burst.

If, as a politician, you're determined to fail, simply trust that the public will vote for you based on your enviable IQ, your brilliant ideas and your watertight arguments. There's no way that will happen, of course – your far stupider rivals will win the election instead. Why? Because they smile sweetly from their posters, churn out hackneyed sayings and go around tirelessly shaking hands and kissing babies.

Want to make sure your next negotiation with a potential business partner is a complete disaster? Simply pore over the contents of the contract, as solemn as a judge, without ever asking them about their wife, kids, hobbies or holiday plans.

But the most tragic failure of all, dear reader, happens when you believe that you personally are a rational being. This deluded belief will make you blind to the fact that you constantly overestimate yourself, get overly attached to your own ideas and keep putting off unpleasant but important matters under the pretext of some (irrational) 'reason' or other.

The quiet voice of reason

For a long time, economists approached their work based on the ideal image of the 'rational man' or 'Homo economicus'. Scientists assumed that people would always reason thoroughly, had unlimited willpower, would only maximize their own wealth, could think lightning fast and always possessed all the facts. This misconception led to the many useless forecasts for which the field of economics was long notorious. But in the 1970s came a shift in thinking. Systematic deviations from rationality were detected with increasing frequency. Economists discovered psychology, which, at the same time, was changing for the better. The field had long been a bundle of unqualifiable claims (think: Sigmund Freud), but now it was becoming established as an empirical science. Today we know what people have always intuitively known, i.e., that people rarely behave rationally. To put it another way: if you proceed from the assumption that people are rational, you'll find yourself constantly running up against walls.

People may not act according to the principles of logic, but that doesn't mean their behaviour cannot be predicted. The rules for predictions are just a little more complex than when we start from a basis of rationality. Most of these rules we acquire automatically, like our mother tongue – but not all of them. If you aren't naturally blessed with an exquisitely keen sense for people, you'll have to consciously delve into the field of 'human studies'. My advice to anyone who is starting out in their career is: read a social psychology textbook. It'll take you a few weeks to get through it, but you'll reap the rewards with invaluable insights into other people's motives and behavioural patterns. This information will come in handy throughout your life, both professionally and personally. It will also help you to construct a kind of psychological anti-manipulation firewall. You'll become less susceptible to advertising, plus you'll recognize your adversary's negotiation tactics early on. Remember, we human beings often operate like lawyers: first, we take up our stance (or more accurately, our emotions, our gut feeling and our unconscious do this for us), then we retrospectively elaborate the arguments that support it.

Once you're aware of this irrational bias, you'll meet your instincts with scepticism. The sooner you accept that human beings are not rational – you included – the better equipped you'll be to deal with them (and with yourself). It would be irrational not to accept irrationality as part of life.

SEE ALSO **Have High Expectations** (ch. 5); **Get Rich Quick, Get Smart Quick** (ch. 35); **Join a Cult** (ch. 43)

30

GET NIHILISTIC

Be quiet for ten minutes and contemplate the meaninglessness of the universe. Matter was formed 17.8 billion years ago after the Big Bang. Gravity pulled this matter together to form stars, which began to glow. Around those stars formed planets, one of which we call Earth. Life soon began to sprout on our planet. Millions of species emerged and disappeared. No matter what we do, in the next 10 billion years the sun will expand and destroy all life on Earth. Even if there was a way to escape our solar system, at some point the last star will go out anyway, leaving darkness to prevail for all eternity. In a few trillion years, the universe will consist of nothing but empty space and black holes that radiate their mass away over time. However you look at it, life doesn't stand a chance.

Pretty bleak prospects, right? You see, cosmically speaking, dear reader, what you do with your life isn't even remotely important.

Nothing lasts for ever. Your love letters, your holiday home, your fleet of Porsches, your children and grandchildren – not the slightest trace of your existence will survive the end of days. All of it will be gone, even your hopes and dreams – all up in smoke, all for nothing. That's the truth, plain and simple. It makes sense to get nihilistic sooner rather than later. That way, you won't have to wait until everything goes to the dogs; you can start feeling wretched right away.

Some wise guys in the past – the existentialists, for instance, figures like Sartre and Camus – acknowledged the meaningless of the cosmos but argued that the key is to find meaning in the small things in life. For these philosophers, human actions are at the root of all meaning. But if the universe itself is meaningless, then why should the little things we do on this tiny spinning piece of rock we call Earth matter? Are you really going to fall for what these marketers of meaning are telling you? Sartre and Camus's arguments are illogical. Life has no inherent purpose or value.

Not convinced? Suppose you're a heart surgeon at the university hospital and are feeling proud of all the lives you've saved – 2,678 in total. That's no small feat! But what if you didn't exist? Well, then another surgeon would be doing your job instead. Maybe they would have saved even more lives than you. Accept it: all of us – you as much as me – are completely replaceable, completely irrelevant. If you didn't exist, your partner would have found someone else to spend their days with; perhaps someone better than you. Be honest with yourself and admit it's true. Go on: every morning when you get up, tell yourself that all things considered, your exist-ence is completely insignificant.

The quiet voice of reason

Up until the nineteenth century, there were four 'metanarratives' that gave us meaning: God, the Enlightenment, nationalism and communism. The philosopher Friedrich Nietzsche was the first to anticipate the decline of these metanarratives. For the majority of people in Western societies, this collapse only became palpable in the mid twentieth century. Today, 40 per cent of Americans say they haven't found a 'satisfying life purpose'. The figure is likely to be similarly high in Europe.

Is there a remedy for this epidemic of meaninglessness? Well, there are various paths you can choose here. You can despair at the absence of any external source of meaning, become a nihilist and slide into a depression – not a good path. Or you can become a cynic, a popular choice among second-rate journalists. Alternatively, you can call off the search for greater meaning in life and strive for a simpler form of happiness, through consumerism and entertainment. As an astonishingly effective short-term solution, the latter is the most trodden path.

The path I recommend, however, is to do something with your skills. Carve out a circle of competence for yourself and become a master of it. Whatever you do, it'll still be pointless in the grand scheme of the cosmos. But by working hard to acquire superior skills, you'll at least end up with something valuable to offer the world (for as long as it still exists, at least). You'll be creating value – not just for yourself, but also for others. This is what the existentialists meant when they talked about finding meaning in the everyday. A stopgap solution that delivers on its promises. There might not be fireworks, but at least you'll find a spark of meaning, even without the explosion. You don't have to be a Marie Curie, Aristotle, Edison or Einstein to discover this kind of meaning in the everyday. While on a visit to the NASA headquarters in 1962, President John F. Kennedy came across a janitor in a hallway and stopped to ask him what his role was at NASA. Instead of answering, 'I clean the toilets,' the manjanitor replied that he was 'helping to put a man on the moon'.

SEE ALSO **Be Paranoid** (ch. 25); **Live in the Past** (ch. 27); **Celebrate Your Resentment** (ch. 42); **Crowd Your Life with Gadgets** (ch. 51)

31

CATASTROPHIZE

Got a bit of a headache? Must be a life-threatening brain tumour! Slight pressure in your chest? Clearly a heart attack. Your partner isn't answering your calls? They're probably in bed with someone else, or maybe there's been a horrific car accident. Catastrophizing – blowing up doubts to gigantic proportions – is a sure-fire way to turn you into a bundle of nerves. May the gloomy life commence!

The objective way to assess risks is to take a look at the base rates, i.e., the fundamental statistical distributions. What is the exact probability of someone dying in a car crash in the next 24 hours? In Switzerland, where I live, it's 0.00002 per cent. The probability that your partner has switched their phone to silent or dropped it in a puddle, or that the mobile network is overloaded? Ten thousand times higher. But who can be bothered with complicated sums? Always believe in the worst-case scenario.

Your old friend cancelled your plans for coffee and a catch-up? She wants nothing more to do with you, that's the only explanation. Failed an exam at university? Your whole life is doomed to failure. Missed a deadline? Your career is over. Fluffed the speech you gave earlier? No one will ever forget that slip-up you made. Stocks going down for the third day in a row? Reserve your space in the poorhouse now. Reports of an alpine cow breaking its hind leg in a landslide? No doubt about it, the world is on the brink of collapse!

The quiet voice of reason

People react more strongly to negative things than to the positive things in life. But why? Because negative things can kill us, whereas the most that positive things can do is make us happier. At one time, there would have been hunters and gatherers who paid no mind to ominous signs – the kind who waved cheerfully at the sabre-toothed tiger when it came bounding around the cave wall. But these sorts of people have largely vanished from the gene pool. It was the scaredy-cats, the overthinkers and the worry warts who survived. We are their successors; their cautious traits are the only reason we're still here.

This principle is harnessed by the media: negative headlines are by far the most effective at piquing the interest of readers, listeners and spectators (which is why we shouldn't constantly consume the news). This phenomenon is known as 'negativity bias'. It's hardly surprising that 80 per cent of all news stories deal with negative content, because that's what generates sales.

As with all rules for human behaviour, it's always a matter of striking the right balance. People who never take negative news seriously are bound to naïvely sail into disasters – financially, at work, in their relationships. But life is equally as wretched for those who blow up every negative news story to disastrous proportions. Catastrophizers, who take every tiny mishap as proof of an eternally valid law of nature, make life particularly hard for themselves. So put catastrophizing on your not-to-do list. Yes, bad things happen. But compared to the positive things in life, they are grossly outnumbered. Oh, and by the way, catastrophizing is not the same as paranoia. Paranoid people see indications of plotting – i.e. ill intent – all around them, whereas catastrophizers simply always anticipate the worst.

Why does catastrophizing lead to a miserable life? Because it's a waste of precious brain capacity. Only when you can also say, 'It's no big deal!' with equal conviction should you allow yourself to do the opposite. People who catastrophize also make overly cautious decisions. If you take risk-avoidance to the extreme and let 100 per cent of your savings sit in your bank account, you'll be guaranteed returns of 0 per cent (or even a loss after inflation). But if you passively invest your money in a reasonably intelligent way, then historically speaking you can expect yields of around 10 per cent per year, despite all the usual fluctuations. But be careful: if you catastrophize and sell your very passive index funds in a panic during every downturn, you're bound to lose money.

If you're pathologically prone to catastrophizing, make an appointment with your doctor. There are various reasons for this behaviour, all of which can be treated – and don't worry: a brain tumour isn't one of them.

SEE ALSO **Have High Expectations** (ch. 5); **Set the Wrong Goals** (ch. 11); **Be Paranoid** (ch. 25); **Never Suffer** (ch. 38)

32

CONSIDER MONEY UNIMPORTANT

If you want a truly dismal life, take my advice: don't waste a single thought on money. You see, money comes and goes. Anyone who thinks long and hard about their finances hasn't understood the point of life. Don't worry your head if you're running low on funds. Just relax and hover around the break-even point – you'll be in good company if you do. Important figures, including most of the founding fathers of religion, scorned money in the past. We don't have to take this life all that seriously anyway; the next life is what counts. As everyone knows, there's no central bank in the afterlife. Filthy lucre is also politically suspect: money is at the root of all injustice, it represents the oppression of labour by capital and leads to alienation. In short: it is the devil's work.

It may well be that your friends are poor and you feel embarrassed about having money, not to mention accumulating it. Poor is cool. Poor is endearing. With your indifference to matters of finance, you're letting people know that you're fundamentally trust-worthy – a trait that many human beings lack. This, and not money, is exactly what makes you truly special. It's this trait that puts you above all those who actually know their bank balance. Another thing I recommend is using hope as a strategy. When you really need money, just hold fast and it'll fall from the sky, the same way you can count on it to rain. Who knows, maybe you'll even hit the big time! Someone might discover you when you're waiting for the bus or working as a barista at Starbucks and offer you the chance of a career in Hollywood. And even if that doesn't happen, you can always bank on the generosity of strangers, rich people, charitable foundations and the state. Did your grandmother always tell you to save for a rainy day? Nonsense. Maybe that was the way they did it in the last century, but not any more.

The quiet voice of reason

The Swiss author Max Frisch penned some wonderful passages on the subject of money. Fondly remembering his lover and fellow wordsmith Ingeborg Bachmann, he wrote: 'I think of Ingeborg, his lover and fellow wordsmith and her attitude toward money. A handful of banknotes, a fee, made her as happy as a child, and then she would ask me what I wanted. Money was there to be used. And the way she spent it – not as a reward for work done, but as something from the privy purse of a duchess, if often an impoverished one …

Her money, my money, our money? One either had it or one hadn't, and when it didn't stretch she was amazed, as if the world had lost its senses … She bought shoes as if for a millipede.'

Perhaps you think Ingeborg seems rather charming – I do too! But sadly, she had the wrong idea. Money isn't there to be used. Money is there to be saved. Only when saved does it unfurl its most potent effect: peace of mind. Savings are like a firewall that protects against economic disasters. Money also gives you freedom by the bucketload. Do yourself a favour and get yourself a financial cushion.

Are you familiar with the concept of 'fuck you' money? Sounds pretty dramatic, but it makes sense. The expression refers to the last two words you'll hurl at your boss right before you leave. It's about having the freedom to quit in order to look for a more suitable job at your own pace. In concrete terms, you should have enough savings to be able to keep your family afloat financially for 12 – or ideally 24 – months without any external income. Another thing to remember is that you can get your money to work for you. Even though interest rates and dividend yields are low right now, there are always returns to be had. A few thoughts on this below.

One: it's particularly important to take your finances seriously when you're in the early days of your career, when you don't have a family yet, when your expenses are still relatively low and you don't need as much comfort. This easy period in your life is exactly the right time to start building up your 'fuck you' fund – before the cost of living explodes for you.

Two: once your financial buffer is in place and you've secured yourself some peace of mind, if you find that there's a little money left every month, cash it in for time. With children and advancing age, you'll find that time becomes an increasingly valuable resource – because unlike money, it isn't something you can't multiply.

Three: stay debt-free. Mortgages are the only exception here. No microcredit. No small loans. No credit card debts. No leasing. If you can't afford a new car with your savings, get yourself a used model that's in your price range. I didn't even buy my own house until I was able to buy it outright – a radically old-fashioned approach, I know.

Think of money as being as important as your health. It won't buy happiness, that much is true. But having no money at all makes for an extremely unhappy life.

SEE ALSO **Trust Your Banker** (ch. 24); **Get Rich Quick, Get Smart Quick** (ch. 35); **Trade Your Reputation for Money** (ch. 37)

33

CULTIVATE A VICTIM MENTALITY

You hear a crunching sound and your car comes to a halt. You step out of the vehicle effing and blinding, only to realize that you've driven into a post. If you're aiming for a life of misery, point your finger at anything and anyone else, just not at yourself. The car manufacturer should have fitted a parking sensor. It's the council's fault for sticking the post in the most stupid place conceivable. Your boss is also to blame; he's been stressing you out so much that mentally you were already in the office. Then there's your driving instructor, of course – he clearly failed to teach you properly.

My advice for a dismal existence is to luxuriate in the victim marinade. Viewing yourself as a victim is soothing, but it also acts like a drug. This mindset makes you feel so much better to begin with, then it quickly gets you hooked. It makes you feel light because it relieves you of all responsibility. Flunked your A levels? Logically, this could only be down to useless teachers and unfair grading. Anyway, exams are just a way of getting at headstrong characters like you.

To become a master of self-pity, you must actively search for prejudice (referred to more recently as 'bias') everywhere you look. This way, you'll have carte blanche to make demands at the top of your voice. After all, society owes you something now. So instead of working on yourself, fritter your time away by drawing up mental scoreboards to prove that 'you' or 'your people' are victimized in every area. Your life will be littered with posts that you're bound to drive right into at every turn. One long, endlessly repeating car crash.

The quiet voice of reason

No matter how smart or successful you might be, you're going to suffer setbacks. Behind the facade of even the most perfectly staged celebrity life, tears still flow. It's important to expect a certain amount of failure in life. If it hasn't happened to you yet, it'll come soon enough.

There are always reasons why bad things happen, of course there are. Every disaster is the last link in an endless chain of causes. With a little effort, you can trace this causal chain all the way back to the Big Bang. Even our self-induced defeats are no different. Why do we make stupid decisions? Not because we set out to make stupid decisions, but because that's just the way things go sometimes due to a lack of knowledge, diligence or willpower.

If you want a good life, take my advice. First, analyse your failures and see what they can teach you. We learn ten times as much from our defeats as we do from our successes. Second, do everything in your power not to slide into self-pity. As soon as you start to feel like a victim, you've already lost. Why? Because the victim mentality prevents you from taking control of your life. It disempowers you. Feeling like a victim is a completely unproductive mindset. It belongs at the very top of your not-to-do list. Don't let it hold you back.

Objectively speaking, it's not *entirely* wrong to think of ourselves as victims. The truth is, we human beings are victims of our defective genes, our fragmentary knowledge, historical injustice and lousy circumstances. This insight isn't exactly helpful, mind you; it only serves to make life worse. A victim mentality is like quicksand: once you've been sucked in, it's hard to pull yourself back out.

So what's the solution? Build a repertoire of thoughts that make you turn your back on self-pity. Charlie Munger tells the following story: 'I had a friend who carried a thick stack of linen-based cards. When somebody would make a comment that reflected self-pity, he would slowly and portentously pull out his huge stack of cards, take the top one, and hand it to the person. The card said, "Your story has touched my heart. Never have I heard of anyone with as many misfortunes as you."'

Munger, who grew up in the American Midwest during the Great Depression, established an 'iron prescription' for himself.

You'd be well advised to follow it word for word: 'Whenever you think that some situation or some person is ruining your life, it's actually you who are ruining your life. It's such a simple idea. Feeling like a victim is a perfectly disastrous way to go through life. If you just take the attitude that however bad it is in any way, it's always your fault and you just fix it as best you can.'

SEE ALSO **Drink Yourself Miserable** (ch. 12); **Live in the Past** (ch. 27); **Get Nihilistic** (ch. 30); **Celebrate Your Resentment** (ch. 42)

34

BECOME A LAPDOG

Falling in love is such a beautiful thing – why not immediately push it to the extremes? Don't just fall in love; devote every fibre of your being to the person you adore. Become a slave to love! It'll put you in a real frenzy – joyous at first, but then tragic. Long-term misery guaranteed. The British author William Somerset Maugham vividly described this spiral in his novel *Of Human Bondage*, in which Philip, who has a club foot, falls for a waitress named Mildred. Although his feelings are unrequited and Mildred takes advantage of his love for her, Philip just can't fight how he feels. He does everything she tells him to do.

My advice for a life of misery is this: ignore Maugham's cautionary tale. How else will you get the chance to revel in this unhealthy obsession? Cultivate a constant fear of being abandoned by the love of your life. Keep them from leaving at all costs; no sacrifice is too great. Perhaps they don't like your hobbies? No problem, just give them up. Or maybe they don't like the people you hang around with? Distance yourself from your friends. Your family too. If you really want to prove your loyalty to your partner, let them monitor your communications, your calls, emails, text messages. Perhaps they'd like it best if you never saw anyone any more? Easily done: become a hermit. You're supposed to belong to your partner and no one else, right?

This next one's really important: abandon your own ambitions. Your career? Shelved – remember, you don't want to stand in their way with your own agenda. Be tolerant of the constant berating of your appearance and behaviour. A truly terrible relationship thrives on daily criticism and put-downs. Perhaps your partner treats you poorly, betrays you, lies to you or mistreats you? You have to put up with these things; the relationship is definitely worth it. Tolerate everything and anything. That's true devotion; nothing else counts.

If you've found someone who turns you into a lapdog, take my advice and marry them! Persuade yourself that complete submission is the ultimate proof of love. You see, the worst form of marriage isn't the kind that has you falling into a coma out of sheer boredom. Or the kind that makes you feel like killing your partner sometimes. No. The telltale sign of a completely hopeless partnership is slave-like servitude.

Of course, the obvious solution is to run away, which you are free to do at any point. But the very nature of being in thraldom means that the invisible chain – which originally should have been a bond of love – cannot be broken. The slave owner disguised as a partner doesn't even have to be particularly rich, good-looking or cool. Sometimes the primitive is what attracts us. It doesn't have to be a romantic relationship, either. You can be in thrall to a friend, a therapist, a boss, a political party or a cult leader. Don't be fussy about who you appoint as your master – all of the above are equally capable of making your life miserable.

The quiet voice of reason

The kind of love that Somerset Maugham described in his book is an unhealthy love, a dependent, psychopathic love, foolish, insipid, servile. Many authors have depicted similar cases of bondage: Tolstoy in *Anna Karenina*, Goethe in *The Sorrows of Young Werther*, John Williams in *Stoner*, Nabokov in *Lolita*, Ian McEwan in *Lessons* and, if you will, E. L. James in *Fifty Shades of Grey*. These novels are condensed life stories, which basically makes them cautionary tales. Read them while you're still young to familiarize yourself with the theme.

Subservience doesn't necessarily have to be rooted in blind devotion. Sometimes it stems from major differences in terms of status, education, money, age or self-worth. People with low self-esteem are considerably more prone to thraldom. They view the fact that they are in a relationship at all as a form of self-affirmation. But even people with high self-esteem aren't immune to it. One only has to think of Tina Turner's submissive dependency on her violent husband, Ike. View this example as a deterrent. The Yale sociologist Nicholas Christakis delved into what makes relationships thrive or falter. When you feel trapped in a relationship with a partner who treats you poorly, there's little motivation to play nice – you'll likely start mirroring that negativity. On the flip side, if you can walk away from your partner at a moment's notice without any fallout, neither of you has much reason to invest. The relationship quickly fizzles out. The sweet spot, he found, is when leaving isn't easy but isn't off the table either. This middle ground gives both partners just enough skin in the game to keep working on, and enjoying, a truly satisfying relationship.

As soon as you get even a hint that you're becoming a lapdog, get out of the relationship. No relationship at all is a thousand times better than being someone's slave.

SEE ALSO **Be Unreliable** (ch. 3); **Get Stuck in Your Career** (ch. 20); **Say Yes to Everything** (ch. 50)

35

GET RICH QUICK, GET SMART QUICK

An acquaintance offers you the chance to invest in a copper mine in Africa. The returns are phenomenal: he's increased his money tenfold in the last three years. It's a safe bet too, as the world always needs copper. A day later, your banker calls you. The bank has set up a new fund focused on financial derivatives. It's too complicated to get into details over the phone, but the in-house financial mathematicians (all of whom have an IQ of at least 140) told him that investors can expect a return of over 50 per cent. The fund is already oversubscribed, he says, but since you're such a good customer he can get you in through the back door. He suggests investing half of your savings in this fund. If it all works out, you'll be 'financially independent' in three years. That same evening, you get an email from a Belarusian oligarch saying he needs a small, urgent bridging loan. If you transfer $10,000 today, he'll pay you back $100,000 tomorrow. An astronomical rate of return.

My recommendation for a miserable existence: never miss a chance to get rich overnight. In the Land of Opportunity, they call this the 'get rich quick' culture: instead of earning your wealth through hard work, far-sighted saving and prudent investments, simply let the cash rain down on you. Go for it! You'll overtake your friends – just on the way down, not up.

The quiet voice of reason

Boston, 1919. Italian immigrant Carlo (Charles) Ponzi, a wannabe entrepreneur with a criminal record and multiple failures to his name, promises investors the chance to double their investment in the space of 90 days. He's not lying about the 50 per cent return; he pays this out by helping himself to the capital deposited by other, newer investors. It's the perfect illusion of a profitable business. When word gets out about this amazing interest rate, thousands of people invest millions of dollars in his get-rich-quick scheme. But Ponzi's money-making business isn't based on a company that actually makes anything; it is founded on thin air. When the authorities start investigating his profits in 1920, confidence among investors is shattered, the scheme suddenly tanks and Ponzi ends up right back where he was years ago: in prison. To this day, his story serves as a prime example of large-scale financial fraud. That's why these kinds of pyramid schemes are sometimes also known as 'Ponzi schemes'. Four thoughts on this below.

One: if the returns they're promising are well above the norm, assume there's fraud involved. In other words, if it sounds too good to be true, it probably is. Get-rich-quick schemes don't work (winning the lottery or inheriting wealth excluded).

Two: if you don't exactly understand how the money is being earned, don't even go there! Steer clear of things like cryptocurrency, multi-level marketing and high-frequency trading. Don't gamble away your money on dubious deals, even ones that are being offered by reputable banks. These institutions are using complicated products to justify a high management fee, which of course will have to come from your pocket. The American author Walter Gutman was right when he said, 'You only have to get rich once.'

Three: if you can't make head or tail of balance sheets, don't buy individual stocks and shares. You'd be better off investing your money in a very broad-based index fund with an ultra-low management fee. An index fund protects you from making foolish decisions and delivers returns higher than those typically achieved by 80 per cent of financial specialists.

Four: the intellectual equivalent to 'get rich quick' is 'get smart quick'. There are plenty of apps, courses and books out there promising to turn you into an expert in just about anything in next to no time. You'll recognize them by titles like *Be the Perfect Mother in Three Easy Steps* and *Become a Tech Unicorn: Join the Fast Track*. We all know you can't attain mastery or rise to the top of a particular industry overnight. Just like you can't become a millionaire overnight without winning the lottery.

Bottom line: stay away from 'get rich quick', 'get smart quick', 'get healthy quick', 'get famous quick' and 'get successful quick' schemes. The only thing you should really be doing quickly is recognizing fraudulent claims like these when you see them.

SEE ALSO **Feed Your Weaker Self** (ch. 2); **Expect Rationality** (ch. 29); **Spin Multiple Plates** (ch. 46); **Crowd Your Life With Gadgets** (ch. 51)

36

RUMINATE

'Your idea wasn't exactly welcomed with open arms.' 'Let's have another chat about what you're bringing to this project.' 'I'm not sure it's quite what we're looking for.' Ouch! What now? When we're confronted with mild criticism or scepticism, we quickly start overthinking. Our brains switch to ruminate mode. Did I say something wrong? Did they mean what they said literally or figuratively? Was I out of line? Did I really act like an idiot? What tripped me up? Does my boss, my partner, my landlord have something against me? Am I done for? Will I ever get another chance?

If you're determined to turn your life into a mental hellscape, be sure to revisit the situations that have landed you on the receiving end of flippant remarks. Don't just go over the events once or twice. No, replay them in your mind a thousand times, for weeks or even months. Sooner rather than later you'll find yourself in a vortex of anxiety and self-doubt, unable to focus on anything else. Even at the hairdresser's or the supermarket, when you're cooking or brushing your teeth, ancient thoughts and images will keep scuttling around your head. You'll delve deeper and deeper into the chest of old memories, pulling out bygone conflicts, arguments and conversations. Remember that thing that happened ten years ago? What exactly was it he said? Did she really like me or was I just imagining it? But you won't find the answers to these questions – only the path to endless despair.

The quiet voice of reason

'There would be less pain among people if they would desist – God knows what makes them do it – from so busily employing their imaginations in remembering past ills rather than in enduring an indifferent present.' These lines are taken from the opening paragraph of Goethe's 1774 global bestseller *The Sorrows of Young Werther*, a superlative novel about the dangers of rumination. Werther's endless stream of thoughts drives him to suicide. And this, dear reader, is precisely the risk you'll be running should you fall into the spiral of constant contemplation. Three thoughts on this below.

If you notice yourself getting stuck in a loop of rumination, snap out of it immediately. Thinking is like a river. The more water the river carries, the deeper it digs into the landscape and the more voluminous its drainage basin becomes, which in turn makes the river flow with even more water. It's a self-perpetuating process. The more often we think the same thing, the more entrenched the train of thought becomes and the more it automatically repeats itself. This principle is the basis of all learning and repetition. Unfortunately, the same applies to ruminating over things we don't want to have on our minds. But how can we resist the pull? Not by simply turning a deaf ear to the things we don't like to hear (this rarely works), but by taking them seriously. The fact is: you may well have made a blunder. Go over the situation in your mind once – the emphasis here is on 'once'. Not ten times. Not a hundred or a thousand times. Just once. Make a note of what the experience can teach you. That's all you can do. Putting these thoughts down in writing frees you up to forget about the whole episode. You know it's still there to consult if you need it – no longer in your brain, but on paper (or your computer) instead. Your brain will be one unpleasant thought lighter.

Second, if you can't stop brooding even after you've put your thoughts on paper, make a weekly appointment with yourself for an hour-long rumination session. Ideally in the morning – never in the evening. Schedule it in your calendar. Take all your worries and scattered thoughts, then start ruminating. You'll see that you learn nothing you don't already know from your notebook. When 60 minutes have passed, you'll realize that the time would have been better spent listening to music or watching a thriller.

Third, there's another kind of overthinking: ruminating on projects. While this won't plunge you into a depression, it's a foolish thing to do. Suppose you harbour ambitions of becoming a writer (not something I'd necessarily recommend). You might carry this desire around with you for years but fail to do anything about it. This isn't a good way to live. Projects are something you should either realize on a concrete schedule or call off. Anything else is a waste of mental energy and leads to nothing but misery. Bottom line: the quality of your thoughts (and relationships) determines the quality of your life.

SEE ALSO **Be Paranoid** (ch. 25); **Live in the Past** (ch. 27); **Catastrophize** (ch. 31)

37

TRADE YOUR REPUTATION FOR MONEY

One of the many paths to a sorry excuse for a life is to cash in your reputation for money. How far you can go here depends on your social status. If you're a police officer, you can earn yourself an extra mortgage payment every now and then if, rather than disqualifying a boy racer from driving, you slip him a note to meet later. If you're a doctor, prescribe medication that may not be particularly effective or even remotely necessary, but whose manufacturer has invited you to a 'conference' in the Caribbean – flight, hotel and expert fee included. And if you're a CEO, trade stocks in your own company (or give your spouse the right tip-offs). If you want this kind of life, graze on the fringes of the law. The grass is particularly green there.

The quiet voice of reason

Born in 1948 in India, Rajat Gupta was one of the most eminent international managers of his day. From 1973 to 2003, he rose through the ranks from simple business consultant to the top position at McKinsey. After this extremely successful spell, in which he earned millions of dollars, he served on the advisory boards of blue-chip companies such as Goldman Sachs, Procter & Gamble and American Airlines. He was also associated with a hedge fund that traded in the shares of these same companies. He passed on confidential information and made significant gains for the fund in the process. In 2012, Rajat Gupta was convicted of securities fraud in New York. His involvement in insider trading resulted in a two-year prison sentence and a $5 million fine. But much worse than that: it also ruined his reputation and finished his career. Stories like this are commonplace. What can we learn from them? Four things come to mind.

One: never risk your reputation for money. This is always a stupid idea, but it's particularly imbecilic if – like Rajat Gupta – you already have vast amounts of both. You see, this trade-off has a unique quality, in that it only works one way. Yes, you can convert your reputation into money, but you can't change it back. As Warren Buffett once said, 'It's insane to risk what you have and need for something you don't really need.' Reputation is a far scarcer resource than money. Buffett, who built the most successful conglomerate of all time, occasionally writes a short letter to the CEOs of his companies. In 2010 he wrote, 'We can afford to lose money – even a lot of money. But we can't afford to lose reputation – even a shred of reputation.' You see, reputation isn't a commodity.

Two: sometimes you're in a position of power – as a buyer for a major supermarket, for example. As someone who's in charge of budgets in the hundreds of millions, you indirectly determine your negotiating partner's remuneration and career, but as a lowly employee, you only receive a modest salary. It's very tempting to award the contract to the supplier that offers you a kickback. Even if you're in dire need of the money, don't even go there. If you do, you'll be pushing your professional and social position dangerously close to the cliff edge. What's more, you'll be making yourself vulnerable to blackmail. In the early years of my career, I worked in duty-free retail (part of the Swissair Group at the time). In Australia and Hong Kong, I had first-hand experience of suppliers trying to bribe me in order to do business with the Swiss. How enticing those offers were! I often came within a hair's breadth of accepting tens of thousands of dollars – as a young buck, I wasn't short of things to spend it on. Looking back, I'm so glad I listened not to the devil on my shoulder ('Ah, go on, you've earned it!') but to the good little angel on the other side. Whenever you're unsure which way to go, Warren Buffett recommends the 'newspaper test': imagine a major national newspaper were to feature your story on the front page – could you live with it? If not, then keep well away.

Three: the grey area between the legal and the illegal is

enormous. Buffett employs a tennis metaphor here: 'There's plenty of money to be made in the center of the court. If it's questionable whether some action is close to the line, just assume it is outside and forget it.'

Four: in some sectors and professions, it's normal to operate inside this grey area. Sometimes you'll be led to believe that if you're not willing to do the same as everyone else, you might as well not bother at all. But just because something is common, that doesn't mean it's advisable – not by a long shot. If you find yourself in this situation, seek another line of work.

SEE ALSO **Be Unreliable** (ch. 3); **Be Hypocritical** (ch. 9); **Practise Ingratitude** (ch. 23); **Listen to Your Inner Voice** (ch. 28); **Say Yes to Everything** (ch. 50)

38

NEVER SUFFER

If you want to maximize your susceptibility to misfortune and suffering, take my advice: live as sheltered a life as possible. Try to eliminate every source of stress early on. Steer well clear of potential stumbling blocks. Bathe in comfort instead. Keep yourself in a metaphorical glass house for as long as you can. Once you've grown and are out there in the real world, you're certain to keel over at the first gust of wind.

The quiet voice of reason

Jensen (Jen-Hsun) Huang is the most successful entrepreneur of recent years. As the founder and CEO of the US-based graphics chip manufacturer NVIDIA, he embodies the American dream. In fact, he takes the dream to a whole new level: from Taiwanese immigrant to multibillionaire. While delivering a speech to students at Stanford University in March 2024, he made some rather outlandish remarks: 'I think one of my great advantages is that I have very low expectations … People with very high expectations have very low resilience. And unfortunately, resilience matters in success. I don't know how to teach it to you except for: I hope suffering happens to you! … Greatness is not intelligence, as you know. Greatness comes from character. And character isn't formed out of smart people, it's formed out of people who have suffered … And so if I could wish upon you … for all of you Stanford students, I wish upon you, you know, ample doses of pain and suffering.' Laughter rippled through the audience. Ample doses of pain and suffering? Not exactly what you expect when you enrol at Stanford, one of the most prestigious universities in the world.

Howard Schultz, the legendary leader behind the global Starbucks brand, grew up in a poor family in a residential project in Brooklyn, New York. His father, a truck driver and war veteran, had to muddle through with poorly paid jobs, which landed the family in precarious financial circumstances when he injured himself at work. A difficult youth, you might say – but it gave Schultz the drive he needed to escape poverty, no matter what.

J. K. Rowling was a single mother living on benefits. She could have made do with a conventional, secure job to guarantee financial stability for her family. But she decided to write instead, resulting in one of the most successful book series in history, *Harry Potter*.

There are thousands of other examples of people who have

fought their way through adversity and hit the big time – not *in spite of* their struggle, but *because* of it.

Of course, there are also high flyers who come from wealthy, sheltered homes, the kind of people who don't have to struggle through hard times. But they are more common among hired CEOs than entrepreneurs. I know many youngsters with well-off parents who have barely suffered at all and are now studying at some of the best universities in the world. These are precisely the people Jensen Huang was talking about in his Stanford speech. The sheltered life they lead is dangerous because they have never learned how to battle on when the world takes a sudden and dramatic turn.

Huang's insights overlap with the principles of Stoicism. The Stoic school, also known as Stoa, is a philosophical doctrine that originated in Ancient Greece and was later developed in Rome. The Stoics believed that a person's true character only matures in times of crisis. My favourite philosopher, Epictetus, went to the school of hard knocks. He was born a slave; his name means 'acquired'. His leg was broken by his master one day (why, we don't know), leaving him with a limp for the rest of his life. It was only later, when Emperor Nero died, that Epictetus gained his freedom and founded his own school of philosophy. Its approach to dealing with harsh fates is wiser than any other school of thought.

Like a soldier preparing for physical and mental exertion, you can use the challenges of life to hone your character. Setbacks are part of everyday life in the business world. People who have already survived a number of difficult situations know how to handle themselves. They tend to tackle future problems more calmly instead of immediately flipping out. This is the resilience boost we get from 'pain and suffering'. It works a treat – at least when the suffering is only temporary.

Dear reader, I wish upon you fleeting, gentle but invigorating doses of suffering. Follow the Stoics' example: don't wait for fate to strike; push yourself to do something outside of your comfort zone once in a while. Fast for a few days, or sleep on the bare hard ground. Brace yourself for worse to come – one day, it surely will.

SEE ALSO **Be a Quitter** (ch. 8); **Set the Wrong Goals** (ch. 11); **Get Stuck in Your Career** (ch. 20); **Cultivate a Victim Mentality** (ch. 33)

39

LET YOUR EMOTIONS DEFINE YOU

Are you livid? Show it! Let it all out. Bang your fist on the table. Smash a glass against the wall. Slam into the first pedestrian you encounter on the way home. Better yet: walk past the construction site, tear down the hoarding, grab a sledgehammer and smash everything that's lying around into smithereens. Keep going until you collapse, completely depleted but free of all that pent-up rage.

Maybe you're not angry at all, just sad? If so, crawl away into the basement, bury your face in your hands and spend the whole day there, crying your eyes out. Listen to Beethoven's Moonlight Sonata or B. B. King's 'The Thrill is Gone' on repeat. Only emerge and crawl towards daylight when you've squeezed out every last tear you can muster.

Whatever kind of bad you're feeling, my general advice is this: really go to town on all your negative emotions. Wrath, grief, envy, fear, despair, guilt, indignation – act them all out. Go on, savour them for as long as humanly possible. Don't just treat your every emotional outburst as a temporary feeling; make it who you are – embody that emotion! Be proud of the power of your feelings. It's what makes you one of the great souls. Also, vent your emotions when you have important decisions to make – like choosing a partner, career or investments. Nothing is as sure to lead you to misery as the hysterical voice from deep within.

The quiet voice of reason

Managing our emotions has always been a tricky business. Even the Ancient Greek philosophers recognized that the capacity for reason is what sets humans apart from animals. And since emotions are animalistic, we have to make them submit to reason. This can be done by force of will, distraction, or using what we now refer to as cognitive behavioural therapy (CBT): breaking down emotions with logical arguments. The Stoics understood that anger arises from our interpretation of situations rather than from events themselves. If someone is being rude or offensive, a person with a Stoic mindset won't fly into a rage; instead they will view this as a welcome opportunity to exercise patience and understanding. They will be mindful that the other person is likely acting out of sheer ignorance. In short: the other person is a poor fool for whom we must have compassion. This is how the Roman emperor and philosopher Marcus Aurelius put it in his *Meditations*. The amount of control we have over our interpretations determines our ability to control our anger.

Christianity adopted many rules for life from the Ancient Greeks. The goal, still, was to keep one's emotions in check. A new anger-management mantra came along: 'And forgive us our trespasses, as we forgive those who trespass against us.'

It wasn't until the Romantic era that this powerful culture of control began to unravel. For about a hundred years now – at least in the West – it has become the norm to indulge in our emotions. We put them on show, we live for them and proudly parade them. We spread them all around, non-stop, sometimes for weeks on social media, sometimes for years on the therapist's couch. The modern metaphor for emotions is that of a pot bubbling away on the stove and increasingly threatening to boil over the longer the lid stays on. Better to vent a little steam at every opportunity!

New research, however, shows that venting and letting rip don't do us any good. The American academics Sophie L. Kjaervik and Brad J. Bushman reviewed and summarized 154 studies on this subject. Their verdict was clear: if we let it all out – chop wood, go for a run, hit a punchbag or hurl plates against a wall – this only serves to further inflate our negative emotions. This applies to men and women of all ages. Techniques that calm us down, on the other hand, do work. So does CBT. All of this confirms what the Ancient Greeks already knew.

Here's a tip: view your negative feelings like the weather. Clouds come and go. Just as you can't switch off the weather, nor can you switch off your emotions. Don't take them too seriously, and never let them define you. Recognize that they are only temporary and don't form part of your identity. They don't even belong to you. But what if, despite all this, you're still fascinated by feelings? Then take more interest in other people's emotions than your own, please.

SEE ALSO **Never Be Playful** (ch. 21); **Listen to Your Inner Voice** (ch. 28); **Say Everything You Think** (ch. 45)

40

TRY TO END IT ALL

Plagued by feelings of pain and hopelessness? Can't see a way out? Well, there's one thing you *could* do: jump off a tall building. Just remember that instead of ending it all, you might survive the fall and wake up in intensive care …

The quiet voice of reason

Sometimes people want to just disappear from this world. It's a familiar story: they go through too much misfortune, too much suffering, too much misery, and at some point they just can't take it any more. Suicide feels like the only option. A few years ago, one of my friends, the CEO of a major corporation, hanged himself. He was in the prime of his life; he was successful, smart, athletic and good-looking, and his employees loved him. But mentally he was stuck in a deep black hole caused by feelings of guilt following an affair. Unable to see a way out of his despair, he finally reached for the noose. Such a huge loss for the hundreds of people who knew him, appreciated him and loved him. I'm convinced that if he could only have stuck it out for a few more weeks, the storm would have passed and he would eventually have crawled out of that hole and lived for at least another 40 (probably wonderful) years. That's the curse of suicide: there's no way to press rewind. You can only kill yourself once.

Before your thoughts venture into the realm of suicide, please remember that we human beings are bad at making predictions. We're well and truly terrible at guessing how we're going to feel in the future. If you believe that your future life will be nothing but one long trek through the dirt, you're almost certainly wrong. Dan Gilbert, professor of psychology at Harvard University, calls this 'affective forecasting'. Here's an example: you've hit rock bottom and are absolutely convinced that you'll never find happiness again. This impression is your brain exaggerating. We systematically overestimate the intensity and duration of our future emotions. Think about it: in most situations, the world starts to look better again after just a few months. Moreover, your personality is always changing, albeit very slowly. In 10, 20 or 30 years from now, you'll be a different person. You'll have different priorities, different feelings, different thoughts. You'll see the world differently. So you see, you have no right to kill your future self – no more than you have the right to murder your brother or sister. If you take your own life at 40, you'll simultaneously be killing the person you would have become at the age of 50, 60 or 70.

Another thing to consider is how much pain suicide causes – and that two-thirds of all suicide attempts are unsuccessful. Chances are, you'll survive with a damaged body or an impaired brain. Think your current situation is miserable? Maybe it is. But there's also an intrinsic upside to life – i.e., the potential for everything to get much better. Maybe you can't see this upside right now, but it's definitely there. After a successful or botched suicide attempt, this upside is obliterated. Trying to prove something? Want to get back at someone? Hoping to make someone feel guilty or set an example? Come on, don't throw your life away for such a cheap trade. You're too valuable for that. Don't do it. You'd be much better off taking antidepressants for a while. They work.

Bottom line: suicide can only be justifiable if you're at the end of your life and there's no hope of things ever getting any better due to serious illness. If this is the case, you should think very carefully. Never act on impulse. Seek professional support from a legitimate and recognized assisted suicide organization. Under no circumstances should you try to do it yourself. And spare a thought for the people you'll hurt with your deed. Think of your family, your friends and the other people you mean something to.

SEE ALSO **Be an Asshole** (ch. 4); **Say Yes to Drugs** (ch. 19); **Get Nihilistic** (ch. 30)

41

MARRY THE WRONG PERSON – AND STAY WITH THEM

Research tells us that the happiest people are those in a good marriage. Single people are the second happiest group. The worst off are those in a bad marriage. If you want a truly miserable existence, take my advice: get married to the wrong person – and never split up!

The quiet voice of reason

There is no decision more important than the choice of a life partner. Choose well, and even if you mess almost everything else up – your career, home, health, finances – your life will still be good, or at least tolerable. Back the wrong horse, however, and you could be excelling in every area but your life will still be hellish. We spoke earlier on about the best way to ruin a marriage. What we're talking about now is how to find this Mr or Mrs Perfect in the first place. Various thoughts on this below.

One (spoiler alert): there's no algorithm to help you out here. Divorce rates would be considerably lower if there was a reliable checklist that you could simply tick off on your first date. What we're talking about here is an almost impossible task, one where chance plays an enormous role. I know some of the most impressive CEOs in the world, and although they're whizzes at dealing with people, they always seem to find themselves in divorce proceedings. The only empirically corroborated factor that increases the odds of a successful marriage is alignment in terms of personality, values and aims in life. The person you marry should be on a similar wavelength and want similar things to you. Why do they say opposites attract? Totally wrong. Opposites are dynamite. Bridging the gap that keeps opening up between the sexes is difficult enough. If you also have completely conflicting ideas about how to overcome every other obstacle in life, then all I can say is: good luck.

Two: forget about trying to mould your partner to your ideals. It doesn't work.

Three: don't just marry the first half-decent person you come across. You see, when it comes to love, there's a thing or two we could learn from maths. One such lesson comes from the 'secretary problem'. It goes like this: you're looking to hire a secretary (sorry, an assistant) and have received 100 applications for the role. You can only interview each applicant once and have to decide whether to reject or hire them. What to do? The optimal strategy is to interview the first 37 applicants and systematically reject them all. Keep going, then appoint the first applicant who outperforms the best of the 37 candidates you've interviewed so far. But what does this mean in terms of finding a life partner? Before committing yourself to one person, you should wait until you've had plenty of dates and relationships to give you a sense of the quality of the candidates available on the market. Two or three random samples won't suffice.

Four: never marry for money. The billionaire Warren Buffett said, 'I think that's kind of a crazy way to live. It's probably a bad idea under any circumstances, but absolute madness if you are already rich.' The fewer other qualities a person possesses, the brighter their money shines. This is the halo effect that we came across earlier. Don't let yourself be dazzled by it, under any circumstances.

Five: how do you find a good life partner? You have to earn the privilege. You too must be an attractive proposition on the marriage market, otherwise barely anyone will be interested in you. Good partners aren't blind or stupid. Before anything else, try working on yourself.

Six: if, despite all your error avoidance tactics (no affairs, no long hours, impeccable household recycling practices) and all your mutual efforts, your marriage is just plain exhausting, get a divorce. There's little point in being shackled to each other for the rest of your life, spitting venom, letting yourself be humiliated, hurling plates against the wall or persisting in a drawn-out display of disenchantment out of mere pedantry. Admit that, with the best will in the world, it's just not working – but don't torment yourself about it. After all, as a single person, you'll belong to the second happiest group of people in society – see above. And you'll still be in with a chance of moving up to the first division.

SEE ALSO **Have High Expectations** (ch. 5); **Mess Up Your Marriage** (ch. 7); **Expect Rationality** (ch. 29); **Try to Change People** (ch. 44)

42

CELEBRATE YOUR RESENTMENT

Want to live in torment? Plunge yourself into resentment and bitterness. It's the perfect recipe for a miserable existence. Someone definitely badmouthed you behind your back at some point. Maybe your parents didn't treat you exactly the same as your siblings in every respect. Maybe your rival tripped you up on the career ladder. Maybe you've been through a bitter divorce, a friendship broke down or you've fallen out with your relatives. Reflect on your life and you're sure to find plenty of people who have given you cause to hold something against them. Wallow in self-pity every day. Don't just bear a grudge; nurture it, don't stop feeding those grievances. Your life will become almost unbearable. Nothing in the world consumes a person as ravenously as bitterness.

The quiet voice of reason

All complex human emotions are rooted in our evolutionary past – anger and resentment included. As hunter-gatherers, we lived in small groups of around 50 people. Everyone knew every little detail about everyone else. In communities like these, there was no place for anger to hide, so all fellow cave-dwellers instantly knew when a social contract had been violated. In today's anonymous society, however, these signals mostly vanish into thin air. But the offshoot of rage, silent resentment, continues to simmer all the same – sometimes even for years.

Tip: banish resentment from your emotional repertoire. This might sound difficult, but I assure you it's possible. If you want proof, look at Nelson Mandela. After spending 27 years in prison, incarcerated by the apartheid regime, he emerged without bitterness or the desire for revenge – and became South Africa's first black president.

If that isn't enough to make you eschew resentment for the rest of your days, perhaps the following philosophical argument will convince you. The Stoics divided the world into things we can change and things we can't. Getting worked up about the things we can't change is pointless and foolish. Anything that happened in the past is unchangeable by definition.

When George McGovern lost by a huge margin to Richard Nixon in the 1972 presidential race, he made a few bitter remarks about journalists at the *Washington Post* who had criticized his presidential campaign. Three months later, he wrote to the publisher of the newspaper: 'I have regretted that outburst and I have also established that the maximum time I can carry a grudge is about three months. This note is simply to say that I have now forgotten all campaign grudges. It is just too difficult trying to remember which people I'm supposed to shun.' Resentment devours a lot of brain capacity. If you can't silence your grudges altogether, simply give them an expiry date.

Maybe this bit of advice reminds of you of how the Bible calls for forgiveness? Now, I can only speak for myself, but I've found that forgiveness doesn't work – but simply forgetting certainly does. Our family strategy: on 31 December every year, my wife and I take a piece of paper and write down the names of the people we have good reason to be mad at, then we ceremoniously burn it. Our resentment flies away with the smoke – but only if we also admit to at least one thing we did that made the situation worse.

SEE ALSO **Feed Your Weaker Self** (ch. 2); **Feel Guilty** (ch. 22); **Be Paranoid** (ch. 25); **Live in the Past** (ch. 27)

43

JOIN A CULT

Become part of a sect. Subscribe to an ideology, body and soul. At last you've found a worldview to explain everything – good, evil, war, desires, birth, death. After all the tribulations you've experienced in life so far, fortune is finally smiling upon you: you are one of the few people who have really grasped what it's all about. You've been chosen, you're enlightened! Look down from a great height at the ignorant, pathetic normal people who haven't seen the light yet and perhaps never will. Go out and buy clothes and accessories to signal your membership of the clear-sighted circle: hijab, robes, kippa, Mao suit, rainbow T-shirt, high-vis yellow vest, recycled truck-tarp bag.

   Don't worry if you can't quite make sense of everything your figurehead has preached – for instance, the meaning of 'the Trinity', 'reincarnation' or 'a classless society'. You just need a little brainwashing in the form of seminars, workshops and retreats. Go on, spend your entire savings and, most importantly, your whole lifetime on your new community! Even better, become a leader yourself! Then, as a bonus, you can spend your days rattling off the rules of your cult. The more often you go around spouting those rules, the more firmly you'll hammer them into your brain. In the blink of an eye, you'll turn your brain to mush and make your life a misery.

The quiet voice of reason

Ideologies (religions included) are consolidated beliefs. They don't emerge as independent, stand-alone propositions. They are complicated intellectual constructs that have survived not because they are true, but because they are good at spreading.

Ideologies profess to explain more than science can. They are therefore mostly fabrications. There is no way to disprove them through experiments. How would one disprove the existence of an afterlife, for example, or the claim that we are all somehow victims? Impossible! One time, when I confronted a devotee of the Unification Church (a 'Moonie') about her pie-in-the-sky beliefs, her response was, 'That is precisely the difference between reality and faith. Reality is something you can verify, but with faith you have to believe; otherwise, you wouldn't call it faith.' Classic circular reasoning. As nonsensical as it is irrefutable.

Ideologies behave a lot like viruses. Once someone is infected and hasn't been vaccinated with sufficient rationality, the epidemic takes hold and cannot be stopped. In the words of the philosopher Daniel Dennett, 'There's simply no polite way to tell people they've dedicated their lives to an illusion.'

Not all illusions are bad – in fact, some are essential for ensuring peaceful human coexistence. Money, for example, is a fabrication. It can only serve its purpose if we all believe in it. The minute we begin to expose the true nature of the 1s and 0s that lie dormant in our banks' data centres, money becomes useless. Property is similarly conceptual: there's nothing remotely natural about it. The same goes for companies, states and global order. These are all completely abstract concepts. Not to mention human rights: does every human being really have the same value? What does 'the dignity of human life' mean? Where is this worth to be found? Was Hitler really as dignified as my friend who founded a university in Burkina Faso? Oh, come on! And even if we do believe in human dignity, when exactly does it start? At birth? At conception? Somewhere in between? Despite all these questions, human dignity is a useful fabrication that it's important to maintain.

Much of what we believe is fictitious but nevertheless useful. So why not join a cult if it makes us happier? Blind faith can be extremely helpful when it comes to coping with everyday life.

My tip for separating useful ideas from useless beliefs is this: one by one, mentally dip all the ideologies, religions and fictions in two acid baths – one for rationality and another for satire. Ask yourself: are people allowed to speak the truth here? Is it okay to crack jokes about this ideology? Does it tolerate humour and mockery? If not: run! As for the intellectual constructs you're left with, decide which of these you consciously accept and which you don't. Maybe in the end you'll find that you can no longer believe 100 per cent in God, human rights or communism, even if you still want to with all your heart. That's the funny thing about becoming enlightened: once you've recognized useful illusions for what they are – i.e., illusions – you accept them all the same.

SEE ALSO **Surround Yourself with Negative People** (ch. 17); **Trust Your Banker** (ch. 24); **Become a Lapdog** (ch. 34); **Invite Bad People into Your Life** (ch. 48)

44

TRY TO CHANGE PEOPLE

If you want to throw away your life on a completely hopeless cause, take my advice: try to change people. Marry a walking red flag and turn them into your project; you can be their saviour! Then raise your children to be carbon copies of yourself: same interests, same strengths, same personality traits. And of course, you should put your magic powers to use at work. Take cautious but highly competent employees and transform them into swashbuckling risk-takers; send your bookkeeper to sales and the graphic designer to software development. Sisyphus will gladly welcome you into his fan club.

The quiet voice of reason

Is it possible to change personalities? Not just our own, but other people's too? What does world literature – that treasure trove of experience spanning hundreds of years – have to say on the matter? The consensus is unanimous: no, absolutely not! Cue two ultra-abridged examples. In Tolstoy's masterpiece *Anna Karenina*, the protagonist struggles to conform to the social norms governing life for an aristocratic woman. She tries to change her personality, to no avail, and ends up throwing herself under a train. In Goethe's *The Sorrows of Young Werther*, our melancholy hero soon realizes that he doesn't stand a chance with Charlotte, whom he adores. He tries everything: he moves away, pours himself into his artistic endeavours, seeks salvation in nature (very romantic). Nothing he tries works. He winds up shooting himself in the head.

What does the science say? Well, there are five stable and relatively independent dimensions of personality, known as the Big Five traits, each of which has its own adversary: 1) openness (to new experiences) versus reticence; 2) conscientiousness versus sloppiness; 3) extroversion versus introversion; 4) agreeableness versus lone wolf tendencies; 5) emotional stability versus neuroticism. Can we change ourselves on the continuum of these five dimensions? Yes, but only at a snail's pace and with a huge amount of effort. As an introverted person, you can set your mind to becoming a little more extroverted by actually being more outgoing. Maybe you could arrange a party, even though it might feel like conquering Mount Everest. 'Fake it till you make it', as they say. Technical term: behavioural therapy. It's all incredibly slow and frustratingly incremental, but it's not impossible.

With other people, it's a different story. You can't change who people are. External motivation, incentives, pressure – none of it helps. So never get yourself into situations in which you have to change people – you'll only lose. If anything, it's much more efficient to replace people you can't get along with, or to remove yourself from the situation. This is relatively easy in the corporate environment. But in relationships, it's more of a challenge. 'If you want to guarantee yourself a life of misery,' Charlie Munger warns, 'marry somebody with the idea of changing them.' If you're already married, either accept your spouse's idiosyncrasies (and vice versa) or get a divorce. Things get even trickier, are fraught with complexity, when it comes to your children. You can't break up with your offspring, so your only option is tolerance. Your children will interpret your love as acceptance anyway, no matter how quirky their personality might be.

There is one exception to this rule. You *can* alter someone's personality slightly by taking them out of one peer group and slotting them into another. But unfortunately, this only works up to a certain age. The most notable example is when youngsters change schools. Suddenly they make different friends and their behaviour adjusts accordingly.

Why do human beings have different personalities in the first place? Well, this is evolution's response to a constantly changing environment. No two plants or animals are exactly the same. Diversity helps increase the odds of the species as a whole surviving: individual specimens will fail, but others will be successful. Of course, the same applies to people. If we all had the same personality – and therefore the same way of dealing with problems – we would have died out long ago. But why, then, are we so frustratingly rigid in our ways? There's a reason for this, too: the only way we can cooperate efficiently and form stable relationships is if we can anticipate other people's behaviour. To become respectable members of our community, we must be almost slavishly consistent – and indeed, most of us are.

Bottom line: working on character flaws is a noble pursuit. But if this is your aim, stick to your own flaws. You'll have more than enough to keep you busy, that's for sure.

SEE ALSO **Let Things Fall Apart** (ch. 1); **Mess Up Your Marriage** (ch. 7); **Surround Yourself with Negative People** (ch. 17); **Make Other People Feel Unimportant** (ch. 26); **Invite Bad People Into Your Life** (ch. 48)

45

SAY EVERYTHING YOU THINK

Say everything that pops into your head. Voice your opinion – let it out! Be completely honest and open with everyone: your partner, your children, your friends, co-workers, superiors, neighbours, the public at large. Authenticity cannot be caged. Release the chaos into the open, liberating your every thought from the confines of your mind!

Some people will love you for this, while others will hate you. But don't you bother about that. Don't just do it for your own good. Do it for your environment too; allow everything and everyone around you to benefit from your openness. Tell people exactly what you think of them – unfiltered, in the raw. There are so many things people could be doing better in their lives. School them all a little bit – including the person sitting next to you on the train, the sales assistant at the checkout and your kids' teachers. It's your own little way of making the world marginally better – and of making your own life a whole lot worse.

The quiet voice of reason

'The truth is not unreasonable for man,' the Austrian writer Ingeborg Bachmann once said. This may be true – but only in carefully measured doses. There's a reason why presidents and CEOs have press officers. When communicating with the outside world, dear reader, you need to be your own spokesperson. Play this role professionally and congenially. That's right, you don't need someone else to do it. Everyone knows that a spokesperson isn't just going to blurt out everything they are thinking, so neither should you.

'You've lost weight – you look much better now!' 'At least you gave it a go!' Comments like these may be well intentioned, but resist the temptation to blurt them out. The less you say, the better. Try listening instead – it's more interesting. You already know *your* opinion, so let others do the talking. Never say what you think of someone else, even if they ask you for your opinion. Just because someone requests honest feedback, it doesn't mean they can actually take criticism. Once the thread of a relationship is torn, it's extremely hard to knot it back together again. When something has been said, there's no way to take it back. Prize tact over honesty – it's an age-old rule, but it'll save you from ruining your carefully forged friendships and acquaintances, leaving you staring at the wreckage.

The moment you look someone in the eye and tell them where their weaknesses lie, you're going to have a problem on your hands. It'll be your fault when they take offence; you'll automatically find yourself duty-bound to play the therapist. So please, refrain from making offensive remarks – even if you 'didn't mean it that way'. It's not your job to educate other adults.

There's also such a thing as tact between close friends. Even in marriage. I'm fully aware that there are more interesting men out there than me. But if my wife were to constantly tell me which of them she currently finds devastatingly handsome, or if I were to tell her how sexy I think this or that woman is, we would quickly reach crisis point. We both know that there could be other partners for us on this planet, possibly even rather attractive ones. What's the point in rubbing it in each other's faces?

One of the most impressive letter exchanges in literature was published in 2022: the correspondence between Max Frisch and Ingeborg Bachmann. Three hundred letters spanning over 780 pages. In one of the first letters, from 1959, the two writers swore to be completely honest with one another. By the end of the exchange, there had been a whole mountain of misunderstandings and accusations. The relationship had become a tragedy and ended in an exhausting parting of ways.

Literature has simulated this kind of total frankness many times. Nowhere more effectively than in Edward Albee's play *Who's Afraid of Virginia Woolf?*, where husband and wife George and Martha reveal scathingly harsh truths to a couple they have invited into their home. They pick away at – no, burrow into – the wounds of their relationship until there is no way for them to ever heal again.

Total transparency is the death of any relationship – personal, public or professional. It's essential to establish clear rules of communication. Don't worship the cult of authenticity. Set boundaries for how much you personally want to disclose. The only radically honest, completely open conversation you should be having is with yourself.

SEE ALSO **Be Hyperactive on Social Media** (ch. 15); **Listen to Your Inner Voice** (ch. 28); **Let Your Emotions Define You** (ch. 39)

46

SPIN MULTIPLE PLATES

Want to achieve as little as possible in life? If so, I recommend multi-tasking. Start at university: while you're studying, chat non-stop on all sorts of media. That way, you can be sure that nothing will stick in your head. Then later, at work, spend your time on a dozen tasks and projects; start everything and anything, but never finish any of it. Go on, spread yourself too thinly! Flit from task to task – and remain mediocre across the board.

When you're on a Zoom call, read the news or check your emails. Everyone does the same in these meetings, so no one will notice. Make calls while you're replying to emails. During dinner, whip out your phone and have a quick scroll through a few WhatsApp messages. It's hardly against the law! Oh, and forget about travelling for the experience; spend your holidays filming and posting content for your socials. Multitasking allows you to achieve so much – a whole load of superficial, disposable, mediocre, superfluous stuff. Everything you need for a crappy life!

The quiet voice of reason

The body automatically does a thousand things at once without a conscious effort. We grow, digest food, repair cells, kill viruses and bacteria, heal wounds, see, breathe, smell, touch and feel, all while making our way through the world balancing on just two legs. Biologically speaking, every human being is a marvel of multitasking.

The problem comes with the activities we perform consciously. In this sense, we have fallen victim to a genuine epidemic of proverbial plate-spinning. Never before have people tried to do so much at once. In the past, this would never have worked. Of course, a farmer in the Middle Ages could have chatted away to his ox while steering his plough; he just had no hope of getting any response. But now, thanks to modern technology, multitasking is possible. You can put on some music or a podcast when you're driving your car. This will only be an issue if you happen to be tuning in to a hypnotherapy session. You can also make an appointment with your physio over the phone as you're cooking dinner. Just don't be surprised if you accidentally oversalt the sauce.

Although we can do several things at once, we can't create anything while multitasking. There's a huge difference between doing and creating. When we're just doing something, we're in the realm of low-intensity activity. But if we want to create something, we must be fully present and intensely focused.

Low-intensity activities are tasks that don't involve trying to achieve anything out of the ordinary. Brushing your teeth, for example. This is just part of any daily routine. You could say that listening to an audiobook while performing this task is a form of multitasking. But unless you're trying to become the world's best tooth brusher, it won't be a problem.

High-intensity activities (what the American computer scientist Cal Newport calls 'deep work') are tasks in which we aim to excel. With this kind of work, we want to produce something innovative or first-rate. Something better than anything we have achieved before in a particular area. In the absolute best-case scenario, we will do better than anyone else in the world. When it comes to deep work, multitasking is impossible. Spinning multiple plates hacks away at the attention we desperately need to create something new or outstanding. Why? Because every time we cognitively switch to a different task, we are left with what is known as an 'attention residue', a remnant of the activity that previously required our focus. If you're trying to solve a tricky problem and you permit yourself a one-minute detour to a news site, it'll take you a full ten minutes to fully focus on the task at hand again. Whereas if you keep tapping away at the problem, it might feel as if the process is dragging on for ever, but you'll be much more efficient in the end. By doing this, you'll be minimizing the attention residue.

The worst attention residues are caused by half-finished tasks that keep barging their way back into our consciousness. Sophie Leroy, a psychologist who lectures at the University of Minnesota, has researched this subject. She tells us that 'it is difficult for people to transition their attention away from an unfinished task and their subsequent task performance suffers'. Nothing short of scientific proof for what your grandmother used to say: 'One step at a time!'

Handy tip: never start the same job more than once. The same goes for emails. The moment you open that email, make a deal with yourself: commit to replying in one go (or deleting it). By the way, in my experience it's also worth changing your email settings to keep the preview of the email content hidden from the overview, showing only the subject line. Otherwise, you run a higher risk of jumping to the next email before you have even dealt with the first.

SEE ALSO **Drift Through the Day** (ch. 6); **Get Stuck in Your Career** (ch. 20); **Say Yes to Everything** (ch. 50)

47

DO ONLY SHALLOW WORK

In the last chapter we talked about multitasking. A similarly disastrous approach I'd urge you to take if you're determined to fail is shallow work. Concentration is demanding, deep work is exhausting, originality is hard. Why should you put yourself through it? Take the intensity down a notch or two. Only accept work that tends to demand too little from you. Skim the surface in everything you think, say and do.

The quiet voice of reason

If you like the sound of a good life, I recommend shifting from low-intensity mode to high intensity in as many activities as possible. Why? First of all, because you're going to achieve things much faster and perform much better if you maintain a laser-sharp focus. Second, because doing so will help you strengthen your circle of competence, allowing you to attain mastery over time. Mastery, in turn, is the only quality that will guarantee a substantially higher than average salary in this global economy. Oh yes, and third, because a focused life is simply more fun. A low-intensity life is grim.

Here are my three rules for going deeper. Rule one: keep shallow work to an absolute minimum, either by clearing it from your calendar or delegating it. Ask yourself: how many months would it take a talented graduate without specialized training in my area to learn this? If the answer is 'a couple of weeks', make sure you get the task off your to-do list. That way, you'll have more time for the deep work that few people do better than you. Meetings, admin and reporting tasks are classic examples of shallow work in professional life. Try to minimize the time you spend on them and use AI tools wherever they come in handy. Set aside large blocks of time for deep work. Add these to your calendar – and make sure they're fixed and non-negotiable.

Rule two: get rid of distractions. Alter your settings to decide which calls to accept and which to divert. I only let calls from family members and employees come through on my smartphone. Everyone else gets sent straight to voicemail, where they are politely asked to write me an email instead of leaving a message. Disable all notifications on your phone and your computer. No buzzing, not a peep; no vibrations or screens suddenly lighting up. Make your phone (and your computer) a distraction-free zone.

Even something as seemingly simple as reading requires our full attention. 'The concentration, the focus, the solitude, the silence, all the things that are required for serious reading are not within people's reach anymore,' the writer Philip Roth once said in an interview. Prove him wrong! Fellow writer Ian McEwan generally tries to leave the afternoons for reading and says he won't answer the phone between maybe the hours of two and four o'clock. He recalls his experience as an avid young reader: 'if you were reading a book, people would assume you were therefore doing nothing and they were entitled to talk to you. Well, I still battle against that notion … if someone was playing tennis you wouldn't walk onto the court and start engaging them in a conversation. Likewise, I think, reading is at *least* as important as playing tennis.'

Rule three: fully engage, fully concentrate and fully focus, even if it means blocking the rest of the world out. The former US president Teddy Roosevelt was known for his so-called 'Roosevelt dashes': periods of complete concentration lasting anything from a few minutes to an hour, in which he focused so intently that he was unresponsive. He would then treat himself to a short break before his next burst of concentration. The physicist Peter Higgs, founder of the Higgs boson, was so absorbed in his work that when he won the Nobel Prize, the media couldn't get hold of him. When Bill Gates was young, he worked 'with such intensity for such lengths … that he would often collapse into sleep on his keyboard in the middle of writing a line of code. He would then sleep for an hour or two, wake up, and pick up right where he left off.' Managing your attention is one of the core skills you need for a good life.

SEE ALSO **Cling to Your Bad Habits** (ch. 10); **Set the Wrong Goals** (ch. 11), **Get Rich Quick, Get Smart Quick** (ch. 35); **Say Yes to Everything** (ch. 50)

48

INVITE BAD PEOPLE INTO YOUR LIFE

Plants come in all colours and forms: lush, inconspicuous, fragrant or foul-smelling, sweet, poisonous, prickly, low-maintenance species, weeds. Human beings are just as varied. So many possibilities! Invite them all into your life. Do it for your own sake: the motley crew of psychopaths, shrinking violets, manipulators, narcissists, liars, freeloaders and nutcases are bound to make your life more interesting. Alternatively, do it out of the goodness of your heart – because you want to help everyone you possibly can, including even the thorniest of specimens. Either way, the more crazies you let into your life, the crazier (and more unbearable) your own life will be.

The quiet voice of reason

Imagine you're stationed on a military submarine and have to spend three months underwater with 80 other submariners. Space is in short supply. You have to share beds because everyone works shifts. If you meet someone in the corridor, you both have to turn sideways to get past each other. No windows, no separate showers, no privacy, no mobile reception, no Wi-Fi, no private communication with the outside world – and of course, no way of leaving the sub. Then there's the steady thrum of the engines, the barked orders, the smell of sweat. You didn't choose your fellow submariners. You're doomed to put up with each other somehow.

Life for the rest of us is so much more comfortable than this, isn't it? Not just because we have fresh air, mobile coverage and a clean bed of our own. The best thing of all is that we can be selective about who we spend time with, where and for how long. Yet we tend to underuse this freedom. We get into a lather about having to deal with people who irritate us, stand in our way or even wish us ill. But there's really no need.

'Give a whole lot of things a wide berth,' Charlie Munger once said. 'Crooks, crazies, egomaniacs, people full of resentment, people full of self-pity, people who feel like victims – there's a whole lot of things that aren't going to work for you; figure out what they are and avoid them like the plague.' Stay away from the following kinds of people at all costs.

Number one: psychos who are obsessed with the idea that the

world is against them and who take everything you say and do the wrong way. The philosopher Paul Watzlawick illustrates this with the example of the mother who gives her son two sports shirts as a present. When he puts one of them on, she looks hurt and says, 'The other one you didn't like?'

Number two is closely related to number one: manipulative types. These people twist the facts at other people's expense and make them feel guilty. Manipulators say things like: 'If you really cared about our success, you wouldn't hesitate to do this.' Or, 'Is that how you pay me back, after everything I've done for you?'

Number three: narcissists. 'You can count yourself lucky that you're with someone like me,' says the narcissist. Or, 'People should be grateful that I'm even involved in this project.'

Number four: erratic, volatile types. These people will shower you with praise in the morning: 'That presentation you gave yesterday – excellent! Treat yourself to a nice meal on me!' But come midday, they'll take it all back: 'You know, I'm always way too generous with you,' they'll say.

Number five: chronic complainers. Their constant negativity will wear you down. Number six: dramatists who love to pick fights or get embroiled in histrionics. Number seven: pathological competitors; they turn everything into a contest and have to be the best at absolutely everything. Number eight: perpetual victims. Number nine: underminers, people who sabotage you by claiming that anything and everything you do is pointless. 'Forget about your book project,' they'll tell you. 'No one reads novels any more.' Number ten: people with a bad reputation. They will get you caught up in fantastical ventures and lofty plans that are guaranteed to crash. Number eleven: people without a reservoir of goodwill, or with 'zero-based affection' – where you have to keep starting from scratch. The list goes on: hypocrites, liars, cheats, criminals, and drug addicts … .

Luckily, you're not trapped on a submarine. You're free to decide who you want to work with and spend your life with. Though there are plenty of tiresome people in this world, there are lots of wonderful specimens too. Find good people to keep you company, both in your private life and at work. You'll know them when you see them – they're the ones who are better than you in many ways: smarter, more astute, more adroit, more honest, more unassuming, more dynamic. People like that will lift you up. Everyone else will drag you down.

SEE ALSO **Surround Yourself with Negative People** (ch. 17); **Get Nihilistic** (ch. 30); **Marry the Wrong Person – and Stay with Them** (ch. 41); **Join a Cult** (ch. 43)

49

GO WHERE THE COMPETITION IS STRONG

Where is the competition off the charts? If you want to put yourself and your career on a fast track to misery, you must make this your destination. The more oversubscribed a particular market is, the worse your chances of success. Start the hundredth private equity firm, open the thousandth bar, the ten thousandth hairdresser's. Sail close to the wind of competition – and secure yourself a busy, joyless life with a paltry salary. The American investor Peter Thiel tells us that 20,000 actors move to Los Angeles every year to seek fame and fortune in Hollywood, but only 20 or so are successful. Go on, join this hopeful bunch – you obviously suck at maths, but I'm sure you're really excellent at acting. Alternatively, stake everything on becoming an international tennis pro. Well, you've beaten all your classmates, haven't you? There you go! That's all you need to reach Federer's level. Or even better. Oh, and study whatever's currently in vogue – business, creative writing, social media marketing. Not only will this make your studies exhausting, but you'll also end up in a highly competitive job market when you're done.

If you're an entrepreneur, you must stay on top of the latest trends – fintech, blockchain, AI, et cetera. You're guaranteed to come up against staffing issues and challenging market conditions from day one. These are the fields where the competition is so intense that other businesses will undercut your prices at the bottom end and outperform you at the top. From the very beginning.

Lone warriors are in the same boat. These days, there are thousands of semi-professional TikTokers in the world. Most of them don't get past the wannabe stage, and the daily and hourly rates are at rock bottom already. The same goes for photographers, YouTubers and journalists. Become one of the millions of lifestyle coaches or novel writers out there. I particularly recommend opening a restaurant. The competition is insane, the margins are wafer-thin and the bankruptcy rates are higher than anywhere else. In short: for a terrible life, do the same as everyone else. Where could you possibly go wrong? Struggle along in crowded fields – in your career, in your hobbies and when choosing a partner.

The quiet voice of reason

Social proof – also known as herd behaviour – refers to the human tendency to follow the pack. We tend to strive for things that many other people aspire to achieve or to become. Peter Thiel says that it is often 'proof of insanity' when lots of people are all trying to do the same thing. Added to this is the macho effect of competing for competition's sake – which has a sporty slant to it but is completely idiotic. Intelligent people, on the other hand, avoid competition. Warren Buffett, also an extremely successful investor like Thiel, is convinced: 'The secret of life is weak competition.' Another person who confirms this idea is Jennifer Doudna, who was awarded the Nobel Prize for Chemistry for jointly discovering the CRISPR-Cas9 'genetic scissors'. She says, 'I've looked for opportunities where I can fill a niche where there aren't too many other people with the same skill sets.' In other words, give competition a wide berth! 'Competition is for losers,' quips Peter Thiel.

Has success eluded you? This isn't necessarily due to a lack of ability or drive on your part. A far more likely explanation is that you're operating in a market that's flooded with competition. Instead of floundering in the flood, why not try swimming into shallower, calmer waters? Put your energy into finding a niche where you can be head and shoulders above the rest. If you want to know how to make this happen, take a look at what strategic thinkers like Peter Drucker and Roger Martin have to say on the subject.

Don't mourn the vast playing fields of intense competition. Ironically, worthless things are often the most hotly contested. Former US Secretary of State and Harvard professor Henry Kissinger once said, 'The reason that university politics is so vicious is because stakes are so small.' The Argentine writer Jorge

Luis Borges used an excellent metaphor to illustrate this point: two bald men fighting over a comb.

SEE ALSO **Set the Wrong Goals** (ch. 11); **Get Involved in Other People's Drama** (ch. 13); **Never Suffer** (ch. 38); **Join a Cult** (ch. 43)

50

SAY YES TO EVERYTHING

Whether it's giving someone a lift to the airport in the middle of the night, supervising the cake stand at a school function or helping a friend move house on your birthday, always be available. Step in to fill all the gaps that have opened up due to other people's bad planning. Be the first port of call for friends and colleagues who need someone to talk to, no matter how busy or stressed you might be at the time. People will appreciate your selfless efforts – soon they won't even bother saying thanks. Well, it goes without saying that you can be counted on, doesn't it? Give your time away with wild abandon, like a billionaire tossing banknotes into the air. If someone asks you for a favour, say, 'Sure – for you, any time!'

The quiet voice of reason

Giving your time to other people, being there for friends and neighbours, helping strangers – this is all very honourable. Such acts of kindness are good for the soul and provide a sense of meaning and purpose. But only up to a point. Specifically, the point where it dawns on you that you've lost yourself. Biting off more than you can chew is a failsafe recipe for stress. It impairs your own performance, which means it's also bad for other people.

It never fails to amaze me that people don't attach all that much value to time, especially when it lies in the future. They treat it as if it costs nothing and is available in abundance, like air. But the fact is, every little bit of time has its value. This value corresponds to the opportunity cost, i.e. what you could have gained, in the best-case scenario, from doing something else with the same period of time on that particular day. This value doesn't necessarily have to be measured in monetary terms. New connections, deeper knowledge, a trip with your family or simply half an hour to lie on your back and study the clouds can also be valuable. It's up to you to decide what your time is worth to you. The next time you're about to give an hour or two away, ask yourself what the best alternative use of that time could be.

This is particularly hard when the time slot you're envisaging is a long way ahead. I can't tell you how many times I've accepted invitations for meals, lectures or meetings six months or even a year in the future, only to regret it when the date edged ever closer.

If you look at your calendar for a year from today, it's probably still pretty empty. But as you're well aware, today's date was also nothing but an empty space on your calendar a year ago. Assume that 52 weeks from now, you will be just as busy as you are this week. Tip: when an enquiry comes your way, instead of checking your calendar, imagine how you'd feel about it if the event was happening tomorrow. Would you have time for it? Would you be willing to squeeze it in? If not, just say no. According to Warren Buffett, 'The difference between successful people and really successful people is that really successful people say no to almost everything.' His plea to his employees is therefore: 'Please turn down all proposals for me to speak, make contributions, intercede with the Gates Foundation, etc. Sometimes these requests for you to act as intermediary will be accompanied by "It can't hurt to ask." It will be easier for both of us if you just say "no".'

Another tip: practice the 'five-second no'. Spend a maximum of five seconds thinking about each request you receive, and once this moment of reflection has passed, answer no by default – unless the request is clearly important or completely out of the ordinary. Don't say 'I'll think about it'. Never say 'maybe' if what you're really trying to say is 'no'. Don't just dash off an unadorned refusal. Be clear, professional and nice about it. Give reasons. It doesn't matter if your justification is vague. You can always just say something like 'I'm honoured that you've asked me, but what little free time I have belongs to my family.' Everyone understands that.

Why are we so generous with our time? Mainly because we're cooperative mammals. Alone we are nothing, but together we can achieve anything. But cooperation isn't a tit-for-tat process – do unto others as they do unto you. We tend to buy in goodwill by giving other people an advance, but we do so in haste.

'It is not that we have a short time to live, but that we waste a lot of it,' the Roman philosopher Seneca wrote some 2,000 years ago. So: set boundaries. Don't jump through every hoop that is dangled in front of you. And make sure the word 'no' is right at the top of your active vocabulary.

SEE ALSO **Be Unreliable** (ch. 3); **Listen to Your Inner Voice** (ch. 28); **Let Your Emotions Define You** (ch. 39); **Spin Multiple Plates** (ch. 46)

51

CROWD YOUR LIFE
WITH GADGETS

Just look at John's apartment – it's a bona fide temple to technology. There's a brand-new iPhone sitting next to a state-of-the-art Samsung Galaxy Fold, both of them crammed full of apps designed to optimize John's everyday life and propel his productivity to unprecedented heights. Taking pride of place in his living room is a huge 4K Ultra-HD television flanked by the latest games consoles – a PlayStation 5 and an Xbox Series X. Everything in the flat, from the lights to the temperature, is controlled by a Google Nest Hub. The kitchen is high-tech, too: there's an AI-operated induction hob and a smart fridge that checks the shelf life of its contents and compiles shopping lists. Be like John: crowd your life with gadgets! You too could spend your evenings and weekends troubleshooting the latest technical issues as these brilliant devices wreak havoc in your home, their interaction apparently governed by the same rules as a group of toddlers in a playground. Be like John: bark increasingly exasperated commands at your Nest Hub, only to be misheard. Enjoy the tropical atmosphere as the heating gets cranked right up at the height of summer. Savour the ristretto your coffee machine insisted on pouring instead of the long black you actually wanted. Despair as your phone constantly buzzes with notifications from devices requesting software updates or warning of possible errors.

The quiet voice of reason

Pursuing happiness through gadgets is a perfect recipe for misery. The idea that technology makes life dramatically simpler for us is an illusion – let's call it the 'gadget fallacy'. We are celebrating around 40 years of gadgets, most of which came along then disappeared into oblivion – PalmPilot, RealPlayer, Segway, Google Glass, BlackBerry, to name a few. Has this technological wave made life easier for us? Not really – in fact, quite the opposite. More productive? Marginally. My tip: limit yourself to as few gadgets as possible, preferably all with the same operating system. These don't have to be the latest-generation versions either. As a late adopter, you can gleefully watch on as the pioneers battle with their gizmos' teething problems. Keep the number of apps on your smartphone to a minimum, then put them in a folder that you only open when you really need it.

The gadget fallacy can be applied to any aspirational purchases: holiday homes, fancy camper vans, shoes and clothing, home furnishings, sport and leisure equipment. Every purchase promises to make your life easier, more comfortable, longer, happier or more beautiful. In truth, it only does so for perhaps a few hours or days – after that, you'll just be trailing the damned thing around like a prisoner with an iron shackle around their ankle.

Our neighbours bought a holiday home in Zermatt. They planned to spend the school holidays in the mountains – skiing in the winter, hiking in the summer – and to let the house out the rest of the time to cover the mortgage interest. It all sounded great, but the whole thing has turned out to be incredibly stressful. Every weekend, one of them has to drive three hours from Bern to Zermatt to collect the key from the last tenants. After that, the house has to be cleaned before the next tenants can move in. Then there's that long drive back to Bern again … They could outsource all these tasks to a property management company, but the fees are so high that it would no longer be worth renting the place out. In addition to all these comings and goings, they also have a heap of paperwork to deal with: mortgage, tenancy agreements, electricity, water, heating, taxes. The list goes on and on. Rather than a pleasant trip to the open mountain air, every journey towards the Matterhorn is more like Sisyphus's climb.

The research on this is clear: having more material possessions won't lead to greater happiness in life. No matter how much you own, there will always be someone out there who has more than you. Meanwhile, you'll find yourself stuck in an endless spiral of envy. And another thing: the initial enthusiasm for the latest must-have gadget fades like that sugar rush you get when you wolf down a pack of biscuits. You'll be left with a relentless quest for more and more – welcome to the hamster wheel of hedonism. Studies have shown that it's better to spend money on experiences than objects. Instead of rushing out to buy the latest iPhone, treat yourself to a few days away. The trip will make you happy in a more lasting way.

In 2011, Marie Kondo wrote her book called *The Life-Changing Magic of Tidying Up*, which went on to become a global sensation. The key message was this: tidy your cupboards, throw everything into a heap and get rid of anything that no longer 'sparks joy' – clothes, gadgets, toys and gifts that you're only keeping out of politeness. I've done this exercise myself. There wasn't much left at the end; most of it ended up at the Salvation Army. Bottom line: the quality of your life rests on the quality of your thoughts and relationships, not the number of gadgets you own.

SEE ALSO **Feed Your Weaker Self** (ch. 2); **Practise Ingratitude** (ch. 23); **Spin Multiple Plates** (ch. 46)

52

FALL INTO THE CONTENT TRAP

What, where, how, when, why? Soak up information like a sponge! Be 'interested' in everything. Immerse yourself in the endless stream of articles, podcasts, blogs and videos that the internet thrusts into your life. With every click you'll gain a new insight and be that extra bit informed. When the feeling of happiness fizzles out (it only lasts a matter of seconds), simply reach for the next nugget of information and feel the hours tick away. Fortunately, the well of content never runs dry! Sure, you'll wake up one day and realize that, despite your extensive 'knowledge', you've yet to accomplish anything of note. But go on, keep on clicking – because what would life be like without that warm, hollow feeling of pseudo-productivity?

The quiet voice of reason

Content is the new mainstream drug of our times. We have access to an endless supply in the form of books, videos, blogs, posts, tweets and podcasts. YouTube users upload 500 hours' worth of videos every minute. Each day, 500 million tweets are posted on X and over 95 million photos and videos are uploaded to Instagram. A good 90 per cent of this is junk, and 9 per cent of it is so-so. The remaining 1 per cent is ridiculously good. But even this one per cent represents such a colossal amount that it would be impossible to get through it all in a thousand years.

Welcome to the 'content trap'. Here, you'll have the illusion of being productive – you are broadening your horizons, after all! – as you passively consume great masses of ingenious content. Not to mention the mediocre stuff and the trash we only see for what it is in retrospect. Getting stuck into content (even if it's good) whenever we feel like it is a bad idea. We desperately need a strategy to stop us drowning in this flood. Five suggestions are …

One: define your personal circle of competence. This is the particular set of skills you want to master. Content that falls within this circle is relevant to you. Anything outside this circle is irrelevant. Choose wisely. Consume selectively. Don't just surf the endless sea of content. 'Interesting' is one of the most dangerous words in this context. Yes, we know, everything is interesting! You can most certainly spend a whole afternoon scrolling through neurotic teenagers' Instagram posts and learn all sorts about human psychology in the process. But the word 'interesting' opens the floodgates to the content trap. Banish it from your vocabulary and your brain. Consume 'relevant' content instead. Only allow yourself two exceptions: a maximum of four hours a week for top-tier content from outside your circle of competence, to help you come up with new ideas; and small doses of content for pure entertainment, such as an episode of your favourite crime series (even though it won't get you anywhere in your job).

Two: don't consume more than you produce. And what you produce doesn't necessarily have to be content. It can refer to any kind of valuable work. Be strict with this rule: you can measure it in hours.

Three: before you get into your next video or book, take two minutes and set a clear aim for yourself. What answers are you hoping it will give you? In what way is it going to help you achieve something? Approach every piece of content with a hypothesis, like a scientist conducting important research.

Four: don't just lean back and let the content wash over you. Actively engage with it. Take notes, write summaries. That's the only way to make the things you've read, heard or seen stick in your head. A friend of mine, a billionaire, creates a mind map of all the content he consumes. He claims that mind mapping is one of the keys to his success. I believe him. I don't make mind maps myself (perhaps that's why I'm not a billionaire), but I do make a note of the most salient points in a Word document. I store the most important insights on a to-do list, which I review every month. It probably doesn't really matter how you engage with content; the most important thing is to be thorough.

Five: read good books twice. Watch excellent videos twice. Back-to-back. Why? Because when you consume something once, you only retain 1 per cent of the content. If you consume it twice, this goes up to 5 per cent. Five times better retention! Incidentally, the ultimate learning boost comes when, after consuming content, you read it back to yourself in your own words. It doesn't matter who's listening when you read aloud – your spouse, your colleague or even your dog. Because for the main part, your dog won't be the one benefiting; it'll be you.

SEE ALSO **Be a Quitter** (ch. 8); **Be Hyperactive on Social Media** (ch. 15); **Get Stuck in Your Career** (ch. 20)

EPILOGUE:
THE INVERSION METHOD

'On the ceiling of the Sistine Chapel, Adam and God touch fingers. To the uneducated eye it is not clear who is creating whom. We are supposed to assume God's the one doing the creating, and much of the world thinks so. To anybody who has read the history of the ancient world, it is crystal clear by contrast that, in the words of the title of Selina O'Grady's book on the subject, Man Created God.' This is the image that British science writer Matt Ridley uses to describe perspective reversal, i.e. the inversion method. Many things in life become clearer when you rotate them 180 degrees.

In this book, I've been trying to illustrate failsafe ways to turn a perfectly good life into a pitiful existence. What I hope now is that you'll go and do the exact opposite. Inversion teaches us not to focus on seeking out role models and best practices, but to look for anti-role models and common, foolish errors. Learn from other people's mistakes and take time to study failures – your own and other people's. Visit the graves of unsuccessful lives, relationships, projects and companies. I encourage you, dear reader, to take up the thread of these chapters and make your own extended not-to-do list. Keep asking yourself: why did this person fail? This question is just as important as the quest for success formulas, perhaps even more so.

The inversion method has been very beneficial to me in my life. Instead of finding out what makes me healthy, I focus on avoiding unhealthy habits. Instead of pondering how I can be more productive, I identify and eliminate distractions. Rather than looking for ways to get rich, I avoid foreseeable losses. Instead of analysing what makes relationships work, I pay attention to what destroys them. Instead of endlessly deliberating in the hope of arriving at the perfect decision, I avoid the decision-making traps that so many people have fallen into before me. And instead of chasing after happiness, I remove the obstacles that are standing in the way of it.

The inversion method has endless applications. Whenever something bad has happened, don't just ask why. Ask yourself why it 'only' turned out so badly and not even worse. Example one: divorce. Say someone has been divorced twice; why not seven or eight times? Example two: inflation. Why aren't the 2020s anywhere near as bad as the 1920s? Clearly politicians and central banks aren't failing on every front. What are they doing right? If you look for answers to these questions, you'll learn a great deal about what makes for a good relationship, a healthy economy or effective world politics.

Another variant of inversion is role reversal. At a job interview, for example, ask the candidate, 'If you were in my position, which particular aspects would you be focusing on?' Or follow Warren Buffett's example and say, 'If our roles were reversed, what questions would you ask me if I were running your business?' Or put another spin on it: 'What information would you give me to discourage me from buying your business?'

Let's get back to the matter of leading a lousy life. There are some external sources of misery that are beyond our control: tragedies such as illness, war and natural disasters. These blows are infinite in number, and we cannot do anything about them. But the other half of the misfortune we suffer in life is the result of internal factors, i.e., things that we can influence. These avoidable errors are limited in number. That's right, there's little originality in self-inflicted dramas.

At the core of this book is the question: are there certain rules we could blindly follow in order to have a good life? Rules of this kind can be traced back to the monastic communities of the Middle Ages. The Rule of St Benedict (*Regula Sancti Benedicti*) is the most famous example. But even behind the monastery walls, many things still went pear-shaped: everything from disputes among the monks to financial problems, spiritual drought and finally the Dissolution of the Monasteries. Safe to say that even in those simpler monastic worlds, no checklist was 100 per cent effective. How could it be any different nowadays, with so many options and different paths in life to choose from, so many constantly changing preferences? My ten-year-old son, Numa, knew this intuitively. 'You can't calculate your way through life,' he said. 'If you could, you'd spend 100 per cent of your life doing maths and then you wouldn't be living any more.' The mathematician Stephen Wolfram terms this 'computational irreducibility'. In short, there is no overarching theory of how to live. It's just not possible. What does help, though, is inversion: avoiding things that are guaranteed to ruin a good life. And thankfully, we now know the biggest pitfalls.

Another thing that occurred to me while researching life's failures is that people don't tumble into (self-inflicted) misery overnight. Instead, it all begins with one stupid action, then another, and then another. These little blunders accumulate until they suddenly ruin everything for us, like an avalanche dragging us down in its path. That's why it's so important to take remedial action early on. But perhaps even more importantly: the art of living is one of the few areas without any need for innovation. Most innovations – open relationships, digital nomadism, rising up against the prevailing norms – don't work. If you're fond of experiments, do them in a physics lab.

Of course, we can't cover the whole universe of idiotic

patterns of behaviour in just 52 chapters. Entire areas are still to be explored – personal finances, health, career and, quite simply, stupid hobbies like base jumping. The journey by no means ends here.

ACKNOWLEDGEMENTS

I am greatly indebted to the seven outstanding readers who made this book what it is. My first reader is always my wife, the writer Clara Maria Bagus. She took the raw material I produced and moulded it into something more intelligible. But her most important contribution was to drastically cut the worst chapters – of which there were more than a few. The surviving entries made their way to my friend Niko Stoifberg, also a writer, who masterfully polished them. They then passed into the critical hands of my two German-language newspaper editors, Sonja Kastilan, head science editor at *Welt am Sonntag*, and Thomas Isler at *NZZ am Sonntag*, before being published in my columns there. Finally, they landed on the desk of Martin Janik, the superlative editor at Piper Verlag; he has edited all of my non-fiction books. For this English edition, my gratitude goes to the first-class editor Jane Selley and my remarkable publisher, Drummond Moir, who transformed my previous book, *The Art of Thinking Clearly*, into an international success; and certainly also to the inimitably precise Isabel Adey for translating.

I would like to thank Eric Gujer, editor-in-chief at the *Neue Züricher Zeitung*, and Ulf Poschardt, editor-in-chief at *Die Welt*, for making space for many of these texts in their publications. I am grateful to my publisher, Felicitas von Lovenberg, for her faith in this project. And last but most importantly of all, I thank you, dear reader, for accompanying me on this journey.

THE DOBELLI DISCLAIMER

The opinions expressed in this book represent the clearest and most truthful points of view I had arrived at by the date of publication. I reserve the right to revisit and adjust my stance at any time. I may even allow myself the pleasure of self-contradiction. Should I ever revise my theses, I will only do so in an effort to get closer to the truth. Never for personal gain.

APPENDIX

In this section, I have limited myself to the most important quotations, technical references, reading recommendations and remarks. I see myself primarily as a translator of the scientific studies cited, as someone who transposes these findings into everyday language. My goal is to make philosophical concepts and academic findings applicable to daily life. Unless otherwise stated, all quotes are taken from the latest Kindle e-book edition that was available in 2024.

Foreword

'In a vow that students the world over may hope he renounces, Charlie delivered "the one and only graduation speech I will ever make" in 1986 at the Harvard School in Los Angeles. This occasion was the graduation of Philip Munger, the last of five Munger family sons to matriculate at this prep school (originally an all-boys institution and now the coeducational school called Harvard-Westlake).' In Charles T. Munger, *Poor Charlie's Almanack*, The Donning Company Publishers, p.150: https://jamesclear.com/great-speeches/how-to-guarantee-a-life-of-misery-by-charlie-munger.

1 Let Things Fall Apart

The Morandi Bridge in Genoa is also known as the Polcevera Viaduct.

David Brooks, 'The Quiet Magic of Middle Managers', *New York Times*, 11 April 2024: https://www.nytimes.com/2024/04/11/opinion/middle-managers-business-society.html.

Are diplomats rewarded for wars that never take place? Does anyone read their memoirs? The answer is no – with the exception of Henry Kissinger. Democracy is the only form of government that doesn't rely on the perfect set-up. It also doesn't call for a heroic rescue if the boss is out of action or in the event of a stupid slip-up. In a democracy, it's not so important to elect a 'great' man or woman; what's important is that they can be removed from their post swiftly and without bloodshed. Moreover, the pressure to be re-elected means that decisions are continuously being brought in line with the will of the electorate – a kind of political maintenance, if you will.

2 Feed Your Weaker Self

Interestingly, an international movement dedicated to easy living and procrastination does exist. See: https://www.idler.co.uk/about/.

3 Be Unreliable

Charlie Munger quote: Charles T. Munger, *Poor Charlie's Almanack*, The Donning Company Publishers, pp.154–5.

Warren Buffett on the collapse of the Long-Term Capital Management hedge fund: '… the whole story is really fascinating because if you take John Meriwether, Eric Rosenfeld, Larry Hillenbrand, Greg Hawkins, Victor Haghani, the two Nobel prize winners Merton Scholes … If you take the 16 of them, they probably have as high an average IQ as any 16 people working together in one business in the country, including Microsoft or wherever you want to name. So an incredible amount of intellect in that room. Now you combine that with the fact that those 16 had had extensive experience in the field they were operating in. These were not a bunch of guys who had made their money, you know, selling men's clothing and all of a sudden went into the securities business. They had in aggregate, the 16, probably had 350 or 400 years of experience doing exactly what they were doing. And then you throw in the third factor that most of them had virtually all their very substantial net worth in the business. So they had their own money up. Hundreds and hundreds of millions of dollars of their own money up, super high intellect, working in a field they knew, and essentially, they went broke. That to me is absolutely fascinating.' See: 'Buffett's Lessons from Long Term Capital Management', *Novel Investor*, 19 June 2024: https://novelinvestor.com/buffetts-lessons-long-term-capital-management/.

4 Be an Asshole

Charlie Munger's funeral anecdote: Charles T. Munger: *Poor Charlie's Almanack*, The Donning Company Publishers, p.290: https://davidsnotes.substack.com/p/charlie-mungers-commencement-address.

On the Mayo Clinic: Tom Peters, *The Excellence Dividend: Principles for Prospering in Turbulent Times from a Lifetime in Pursuit of Excellence*, Nicholas Brealey Publishing, p.45.

Assholes rarely make it all the way to the top. There's a glass ceiling for assholes too; let's call it the 'asshole ceiling'.

5 Have High Expectations

'Psychologists tell us that in order to learn from experience, two ingredients are necessary: frequent practice and immediate feedback. When these conditions are present, such as when we learn to ride a bike or drive a car, we learn, possibly with some mishaps along the way. But many of life's problems do not offer these opportunities.' Richard H. Thaler, *Misbehaving: The Making of Behavioral Economics*, W. W. Norton & Company, p.50.

6 Drift Through the Day

Why do we find realistic daily planning so difficult? Answer: complex tasks and long-term goals are a new phenomenon in the history of humankind. From an evolutionary perspective, our brains are not prepared to cope with them. Focusing on immediate problems and rewards (such as finding food or shelter) was more important for our ancestors' survival than long-term planning.

The comment about finding a to-do list at a prehistoric archaeological site was obviously a joke; writing hadn't even been invented in those times.

Julia Alvarez quote: in Ariel Gore, *How to Become a Famous Writer Before You Are Dead*, Crown, p.38.

J. P. Morgan story: in Tom Peters, *The Excellence Dividend: Principles for Prospering in Turbulent Times from a Lifetime in Pursuit of Excellence*, Nicholas Brealey Publishing, p.56.

'"Before the rest of the world is eating breakfast," writes Laura Vanderkam in *What the Most Successful People Do Before Breakfast*, "the most successful people have already scored daily victories that are advancing them toward the lives they want." Vanderkam studied successful people and she discovered that early mornings were when they had the most control over their own schedules. They used this time to work on their priorities.' See: Farnam Street Blog: https://fs.blog/what-the-most-successful-people-do-before-breakfast/.

9 Be Hypocritical

Upton Sinclair quote: https://quoteinvestigator.com/2017/11/30/salary/.

10 Cling to Your Bad Habits

John Wooden quote: in Tom Peters, *The Excellence Dividend: Principles for Prospering in Turbulent Times from a Lifetime in Pursuit of Excellence*, Nicholas Brealey Publishing, p.161.

11 Set the Wrong Goals

Given the lack of logical justification, wouldn't it be better to not set any life goals at all? No, because then we'd be making impulse-based decisions. An impulse is a fleeting micro-feeling: 'I like this' or 'I don't like that'. Were it not for life goals, we wouldn't hesitate to do exactly the things we like and avoid the things we don't like. There would be nothing to distinguish us from animals. We would be thrown back to the simple life goal of not dying.

12 Drink Yourself Miserable

On the loss of composure: '... alcohol will take the brakes off the mouth, allowing us to career downhill into the realm of the social pariah'. In Randy Paterson, *How to Be Miserable, 40 Strategies You Already Know*, New Harbinger Publications, p.40.

Swiss statistics: Bundesamt für Gesundheit (Swiss Federal Office for Health), https://www.bag.admin.ch/bag/de/home/zahlen-undstatistiken/zahlen-fakten-zu-sucht/zahlen-fakten-zu-alkohol.html.

German statistics: Deutsche Hauptstelle für Suchtfragen (German Centre for Addiction Issues), www.dhs.de.

There's another main cause of alcoholism besides self-medication: peer pressure. If your friends drink a lot, you may eventually become dependent on alcohol. This is known in psychology as social proof: the more people who display a particular kind of behaviour, the more 'acceptable' or 'right' this behaviour seems – which, of course, is absurd. There are smarter ways to block out your life for a while if it's getting too much for you. My wife, for example, imagines that she's missing certain body parts – that she's blind, deaf or has lost an arm or a leg – and then she thinks it all through again. Comparing your own life with a worse version is beneficial.

On the myth that red wine is healthy, see: Harvard Health Blog, 'Is red wine actually good for your heart', 29 January 2020: https://www.health.harvard.edu/blog/is-red-wine-good-actually-for-your-heart-2018021913285.

14 Only Learn from Your Own Experience

Charles T. Munger, *Poor Charlie's Almanack*, The Donning Company Publishers, p.69: https://jamesclear.com/greatspeeches/how-to-guarantee-a-life-of-misery-by-charlie-munger.

Charlie Munger on reading constantly: Charles T. Munger, *Poor Charlie's Almanack*, quoted online at Yahoo Finance, 28 November 2023: https://finance.yahoo.com/news/memorable-quotes-from-berkshire-hathaways-charlie-munger-225308303.html.

15 Be Hyperactive on Social Media

Walter Isaacson, *The Code Breaker: Jennifer Doudna, Gene Editing, and the Future of the Human Race*, Simon & Schuster, p.356.

The perfect envy machine: envy is one of the most toxic emotions, and you should immediately remove it from your repertoire.

For famous people who have quit social media, see: '39 Celebrities Who Quit Social Media (And the Ones Who Never

Looked Back)', Bored Panda, 2 June 2023: https://www.bored
panda.com/celebrities-who-quit-social-media/?utm_source=
google&utm_medium=organic&utm_campaign=organic#.

16 Indulge in Road Rage

Age is the main factor at play: Nancy Rhodes and Kelly Pivik,
'Age and gender differences in risky driving: The roles of positive
affect and risk perception', in *Accident Analysis & Prevention*
43(3):923–31.

My friend Eckart von Hirschhausen was the one who gave me
this tip about the clown's nose.

17 Surround Yourself with Negative People

The model of the atom with the electrons orbiting the nucleus
(known as the Bohr model) has been disproven. We can never tell
exactly where the electrons are. These days, we speak of a fuzzy
electron cloud based on Schrödinger's wave equation.

Kahneman and Tversky: see: https://en.wikipedia.org/wiki/
Loss_aversion.

The following scientific studies deal with emotional contagion
and the correlation between happiness (well-being) and physical
health:

Hatfield, E., Cacioppo, J. T., & Rapson, R. L., *Emotional
contagion*, Cambridge University Press; Editions de la Maison des

Sciences de l'Homme

Rasmussen, H. N., Scheier, M. F., & Greenhouse, J. B. (2009), 'Optimism and physical health: A meta-analytic review', *Annals of Behavioral Medicine*, 37 (3), 239–56

Boehm, J. K., & Kubzansky, L. D. (2012), 'The heart's content: The association between positive psychological well-being and cardiovascular health', *Psychological Bulletin*, 138 (4), 655

Isen, A. M., Daubman, K. A., & Nowicki, G. P. (1987), 'Positive affect facilitates creative problem-solving', *Journal of Personality and Social Psychology*, 52 (6), 1122

Fredrickson, B. L. (2001), 'The role of positive emotions in positive psychology', *American Psychologist*, 56 (3), 218

Dweck, Carol S., *Mindset, The New Psychology of Success*, Random House

Diener, E., & Chan, M. Y. (2011), 'Happy people live longer: Subjective wellbeing contributes to health and longevity', *Applied Psychology: Health and Well-Being*, 3 (1), 1–43

Interesting point: the brilliant researcher Nicholas Christakis and his colleague James Fowler have shown that negativity not only rubs off on immediate friends but also permeates social networks and has an impact on friends of friends. See: J. H. Fowler, N. A. Christakis, Steptoe and Diez Roux (2009), 'Dynamic Spread of Happiness in a Large Social Network: Longitudinal Analysis of the Framingham Heart Study Social Network', *BMJ: British Medical Journal*, 338 (7685), 23–7: http://www.jstor.org/stable/20511686.

18 Micromanage Your Neighbours

On collective efficacy: Robert J. Sampson, Stephen W. Raudenbush and Felton Earls, 'Neighborhoods and Violent Crime: A Multilevel Study of Collective Efficacy', *Science 277*, no. 5328 (1997): 918–24: http://www.jstor.org/stable/2892902.

19 Say Yes to Drugs

Statistics on drug-related deaths in the USA are from the National Institute on Drug Abuse (NIDA): https://nida.nih.gov/research-topics/trends-statistics/overdose-death-rates.

Chinese empire: measured by purchasing power parity, China's share of global GDP went from 33 per cent in 1820 to 5 per cent in 1950. See the ChinaPower Project: https://chinapower.csis.org/tracker/china-gdp/; and Derek Thompson, 'The Economic History of the Last 2,000 Years in 1 Little Graph', *The Atlantic*, 19 June 2012: https://www.theatlantic.com/business/archive/2012/06/the-economic-history-of-the-last-2-000-years-in-1-little-graph/258676/.

Absurdly, China categorically refused to adopt superior Western technology (steamers, cannons) at this time, while Japan decided otherwise. See Henry Kissinger, *On China*, Penguin Press, 2011, p.79: 'Japan, like China, encountered Western ships wielding unfamiliar technology and overwhelming force in the mid-nineteenth century – in Japan's case, the 1853 landing of the American Commodore Matthew Perry's "black ships". But

Japan drew from the challenge the opposite conclusion as China: it threw open its doors to foreign technology and overhauled its institutions in an attempt to replicate the Western powers' rise. (In Japan, this conclusion may have been assisted by the fact that foreign ideas were not seen as connected to the question of opium addiction, which Japan largely managed to avoid.) In 1868, the Meiji Emperor, in his charter oath, announced Japan's resolve: "Knowledge shall be sought from all over the world, and thereby the foundations of the imperial rule shall be strengthened." Japan's Meiji Restoration and drive to master Western technology opened the door to stunning economic progress.'

See 'Your Brain on LSD Looks A Lot Like A Baby's', NPR, 17 April 2016: https://www.npr.org/2016/04/17/474569125/your brain-on-lsd-looks-a-lot-like-a-babys; reiterated in an interview with Ian McEwan: https://www.youtube.com/watch?v=1mTgH3 KWdR8, time code 33:29.

20 Get Stuck in Your Career

Charlie Munger USC Law Commencement Speech, May 2007: https://www.youtube.com/watch?v=u81l7rM2yl8, time code 1:50 and 1:00.

Learning is more important than intelligence: slightly adapted from 'learning trumps intellect'. In Roger L. Martin, *The Opposable Mind: How Successful Leaders Win Through Integrative Thinking*, Harvard Business School Press, p.99.

21 Never Be Playful

American Gothic is in the Art Institute of Chicago: https://www.artic.edu/artworks/6565/american-gothic.

On research into playfulness, see:

Proyer, R. T. (2017), 'A new structural model for the study of adult playfulness: Assessment and exploration of an understudied individual differences variable', *Personality and Individual Differences*, 108, 113–22

Guitard, P., Ferland, F., & Dutil, É. (2005), 'Toward a better understanding of playfulness in adults', *Occupational Therapy Journal of Research*, 25 (1), 9–22

Barnett, L. A. (2007), 'The nature of playfulness in young adults', *Personality and Individual Differences*, 43(4), 949–58

Magnuson, C. D., & Barnett, L. A. (2013), 'The Playful Advantage: How Playfulness Enhances Coping with Stress', *Leisure Sciences*, 35(2), 129–44

Yu, C., Levesque-Bristol, C., & Maeda, Y. (2018), 'Generalizability and applicability of the revised playfulness scale in a college student sample', *The Journal of Genetic Psychology*, 179(4), 187–97

I got the idea of the dopamine list from my friend Thomas Ebeling.

See: Paul Watzlawick, *The Situation is Hopeless, But Not Serious*, W. W. Norton & Company, 1983, p.85.

22 Feel Guilty

Ian McEwan on the concept of closure: 'Live! at the Library with Ian McEwan: The Journey of Life in "Lessons"': https://www.youtube.com/watch?v=rdJkifRdP44, time code 11:42.

Richard Feynman on John von Neumann's idea of social responsibility: Richard P. Feynman, *Surely You're Joking, Mr Feynman!*, W. W. Norton & Company, p.132.

23 Practise Ingratitude

On the headwinds/tailwinds asymmetry, see: Davidai, S., Gilovich T., 'The headwinds/tailwinds asymmetry: An availability bias in assessments of barriers and blessings', *Journal of Personality and Social Psychology*, December 2016; 111(6):835–51. DOI: 10.1037/pspa0000066. PMID: 27869473.

Chair in the sky: see Louis CK on YouTube: https://www.youtube.com/watch?v=oTcAWN5R5-I.

24 Trust Your Banker

Charlie Munger quote: https://www.goodreads.com/quotes/11903 426-show-me-the-incentive-and-i-ll-show-you-the-outcome.

I wrote about the incentive super-response tendency in my book *The Art of Thinking Clearly*.

Don't be responsible for bringing any stupid incentive systems into the world, either.

This is particularly relevant for politicians. One example is the 'welfare trap'. Benefits are provided to poor people with the good intention of helping them and allowing a degree of justice, but the benefits are so high that it's no longer worth those people working. This makes the situation even more problematic in the long term because they stay out of working life for much too long and their skills atrophy. See https://en.wikipedia.org/wiki/Welfare_trap.

One of my favourite examples of idiotic incentives from the business world is the Federal Express scenario described by Charlie Munger. The problem arose when FedEx were failing to shift all the packages in their main distribution centre each night. Although management made various attempts to solve the problem, the night-shift workers failed to fulfil their duties. This inefficiency led to delays, which in turn disappointed the customers who were expecting prompt deliveries. The root of the problem was in the system of rewards for night-shift workers, who were initially paid by the hour. The breakthrough came when the management team switched to a fixed fee for the whole shift instead. This adjustment gave the employees a direct incentive to finish sorting the parcels rapidly so that they could go home earlier. In Charles T. Munger, *Poor Charlie's Almanack*, The Donning Company Publishers, p.200 ff.

On the halo effect, see https://en.wikipedia.org/wiki/Halo_effect.

Often, we can't tell whether we are caught in a toxic incentive system. This is where an outside perspective can help. Ask a friend; they should be able to gauge your situation.

25 Be Paranoid

Marriage contracts: 'If your proposed marriage contract has 47 pages, my suggestion is that you not enter.' In Charles T. Munger, *Poor Charlie's Almanack*, The Donning Company Publishers, p.304.

On the 'seamless web of deserved trust': in many cases and after a certain period of experience, it is good and reasonable for mistrust to mutate into trust. This is particularly special when it comes to people we work with. I founded the WORLD.MINDS organization with my American (and now Swiss) colleague Kipper Blakeley. Even now, after 20 years, we've still never had a contract. We have blind trust in one another. Quality of life doesn't get any purer than that!

26 Make Other People Feel Unimportant

Active listening: see Susan Scott, *Fierce Conversations: Achieving Success at Work and in Life, One Conversation at a Time*, Hachette Digital, Little Brown.

Ogi's guiding principle was always 'You have to like people' ('*Man muss Menschen mögen*'). See https://www.suedostschweiz. ch/zeitung/adolf-ogi-man-muss-menschen-moegen.

27 Live in the Past

How much of your life should you devote to the past? Charlie

Munger: 'I don't spend much time regretting the past, once I've taken my lesson from it. I don't dwell on it.' In Janet Lowe, *Damn Right!: Behind the Scenes with Berkshire Hathaway Billionaire Charlie Munger*, John Wiley & Sons, p.45.

What's more, our memories are pretty inaccurate. Our brain pieces together a past that didn't happen the way we remember it.

In F. Scott Fitzgerald's novel *The Great Gatsby*, Gatsby accumulates tremendous wealth and hosts opulent parties to reconquer the heart of his former love, Daisy. His extravagant lifestyle reflects a longing for bygone times. Gatsby romanticizes the past to such an extent that the present can never be enough. His fixation on the old glory days reveals him to be a prisoner of the past, unable to open himself up to the present.

Speaking of politics: conservatives are often wrongly referred to as nostalgists. Nostalgia is about wanting to go back to a romanticized past, but conservatism says: we trust in the tried and tested; we don't have to join in with every trend. Nostalgia embodies the principle of regression. Conservatism is all about being cautious.

The colleague who summoned me out of my Swissair nostalgia was Andreas Spycher.

28 Listen to Your Inner Voice

More recent research claims that we have 6,200 thoughts on average each day. I'm not so sure about this figure. It would mean that we linger on a thought for at least 10 seconds before switching to the next one. Try the experiment on yourself. Unless you're a meditation guru, you won't be able to do it. See: Anne Craig, 'Discovery of "thought worms" opens window to the mind', in *Queen's Gazette*, 13 July 2020: https://www.queensu.ca/gazette/stories/discovery-thought-worms-opens-window-mind.

29 Expect Rationality

Investing on the stock exchange: perhaps you buy shares that everyone's talking about at the moment, only to realize later that you've paid far too much for them. Your subconscious galloped after the herd, but you rationalize your purchase with the idea that the shares could be worth twice as much in two years.

On *Homo economicus*: 'Although it is never stated explicitly as an assumption in an economics textbook, in practice economic theory presumes that self-control problems do not exist.' In Richard H. Thaler, *Misbehaving: The Making of Behavioral Economics*, W. W. Norton & Company, p.86.

30 Get Nihilistic

'To Camus, the fact that humans search ceaselessly for meaning but do not find it anywhere in the world renders life absurd; everything – from grand historical events to the great effort we all put into living our lives – seems pointless.' In Emily Esfahani

Smith, *The Power of Meaning: The true route to happiness*, Rider, p.486.

It's easier to enter the nihilistic mindset than you'd think. Jordan Peterson: 'Any idiot can choose a frame of time within which nothing matters.' https://www.goodreads.com/quotes/9 770611-there-will-always-be-people-better-than-you-thats-a -clich.

The term 'metanarratives' comes from the French philosopher Jean-François Lyotard, one of the founders of postmodernism. Then came findings in the natural sciences that were also unable to pinpoint any real meaning – quite the opposite. It really is true that there is no cosmic meaning.

An epidemic of meaningless: 'Four in ten Americans have not discovered a satisfying life purpose. And nearly a quarter of Americans – about one hundred million people – do not have a strong sense of what makes their lives meaningful.' Emily Esfahani Smith, *The Power of Meaning: The true route to happiness*, Rider.

The anecdote about Kennedy's visit to NASA: 'The ability to find purpose in the day-to-day tasks of living and working goes a long way toward building meaning. It was the mindset, for instance, adopted by the janitor John F. Kennedy ran into at NASA in 1962. When the president asked him what he was doing, the janitor apparently responded saying that he was "helping put a man on the moon".' From ibid.

The following quote tells us something similar: 'We who cut mere stones must always be envisioning cathedrals.' Andrew Hunt and David Thomas, *The Pragmatic Programmer, From Journeyman to Master*, Addison-Wesley, p.xx.

31 Catastrophize

Another example of catastrophizing: 'Still seated in your chair, look through the window into the sky. With a little bit of luck you will soon notice a large number of tiny, bubblelike circles in your visual field. When you keep your eyes fixed, the circles will gradually drift downward; when you blink, they jump up again. Notice further that these circles appear to grow in size and number as you concentrate on them. Consider the possibility of an insidious eye disease, for it is clear that your eyesight will be severely impaired once these circles finish covering your entire field of vision. Consult an ophthalmologist. He will try to explain to you that you are worrying about something that is perfectly harmless and normal, namely, what are called floaters. [Now assume, please, that he was either in bed with the measles when this disease was taught to his class in medical school, or that out of sheer compassion he does not want to inform you of the incurable nature of your illness.]' In Paul Watzlawick, *The Situation is Hopeless, But Not Serious*, W. W. Norton & Company, p.43.

On the probability of dying within 24 hours of a road traffic accident: on average, 215 people die from road traffic accidents every year in Switzerland. With approximately 4 million road users over a period of 356 days, the probability is therefore

0.00002 per cent. See: https://www.bfu.ch/de/dossiers/risiken-im-strassenverkehr. For roughly 30 million regular road users per day in Germany, there are 2,800 traffic fatalities, giving us 0.000025 per cent, a similar probability as in Switzerland. https://de.statista.com/statistik/daten/studie/185/umfrage/todesfaelle-imstrassenverkehr/.

The 10 per cent annual return refers to the American S&P 500 Index, the most popular stock market index in the world. Obviously, custodian fees, transaction costs and tax on dividends and wealth must be deducted from this. According to Investopedia, 'The average annualized return since its inception in 1928 through Dec. 31, 2023, is 9.90%. The average annualized return since adopting 500 stocks into the index in 1957 through Dec. 31, 2023, is 10.26%.' https://www.investopedia.com/ask/answers/042415/what-average-annual-return-sp-500.asp.

32 Consider Money Unimportant

As the saying goes, 'Don't go broke trying to impress broke people.'

Max Frisch, *Montauk*, translated by Geoffrey Skelton, Harcourt Brace Jovanovich, p.125. (Original German text: Suhrkamp, *Montauk: Eine Erzählung*, p.193.)

An additional consideration regarding interest: 'Why should my future goals matter more than those I have now? … Why should a youth suppress his budding passions in favor of the sordid interest of his own withered old age? Why is that problematical old man who may bear his name fifty years hence nearer to him now than any other imaginary creature? ... Caring about yourself as it will be in the future is no more reasonable than caring about the self you are now. Less so, if your future self is less worth caring about.' In John Gray, *Straw Dogs*, Farrar Straus and Giroux, p.105.

My response to John Gray: 'compounded interest', i.e., the interest on interest, the capital generated on top of existing capital, makes modern abstention from consumption non-linear and therefore attractive.

If you find it difficult to save money – perhaps because you're not earning all that much at the moment or have lost your job – remember how you lived as a youngster. Your first apartment. What you ate, what you did for holidays, what you spent (and didn't spend) your money on. Differentiate mercilessly between 'absolutely necessary' and 'nice to have'. You'll be amazed at how little you need to get by. Side note: you'll also be amazed at the positive impact that self-denial has on your peace of mind as well as your bank account. And even if this bit of advice arrives too late for you (perhaps because you already have a family), be uncompromising about making sure that you're spending less than you're earning every month – make it your very own 'grandma rule'.

33 Cultivate a Victim Mentality

An example of self-pity from contemporary literature: in his novel *Lessons*, the author Ian McEwan describes 'that refined sense of failure and self-pity for what life had stolen from you'. Ian McEwan, *Lessons*, Vintage, p.463.

Passing the buck is also known as 'blame shifting'.

Suffering setbacks: 'It's ... necessary to accommodate a lot of failure, and because no matter how able you are, you're going to have headwinds and troubles ... If a person just keeps going on the theory that life is full of vicissitudes and just does the right thinking and follows the right values it should work out well in the end. So I would say, don't be discouraged by a few reverses.' Charlie Munger, in Peter Bevelin, *All I Want to Know Is Where I'm Going to Die So I'll Never Go There*, PCA Publications, 2016, p.57.

The economist Thomas Sowell has voiced fierce criticism of the victim mentality: 'Those who promote an ideology of victimhood may imagine that they are helping those at the bottom, when in fact they are harming them.' In *The Columbus Dispatch*: https://eu.dispatch.com/story/opinion/cartoons/2013/12/03/thomas-sowell-commentary-victimhood-is/24035607007/.

There are entire university departments that try to convince the world about victim mentality. This attitude is referred to by the label 'woke'. In the political realm, it is known as 'identity politics'.

The story of the pity cards continues: 'Well, you can say that's waggery, but I suggest it can be mental hygiene. Every time you find you're drifting into self-pity, whatever the cause, even if your child is dying of cancer, self-pity is not going to help. Just give yourself one of my friend's cards. Self-pity is always counterproductive. It's the wrong way to think. And when you avoid it, you get a great advantage over everybody else, or almost everybody else, because self-pity is a standard response. And you can train yourself out of it.' In Charles T. Munger, *Poor Charlie's Almanack*, The Donning Company Publishers, p.297.

Munger's iron prescription: In Janet Lowe, *Damn Right!: Behind the Scenes with Berkshire Hathaway Billionaire Charlie Munger*, John Wiley & Sons, p.224.

34 Become a Lapdog

Nicholas A. Christakis, *Blueprint: The Evolutionary Origins of a Good Society*, Little Brown and Co., p.171: 'Interestingly, we found a parabolic relationship between social fluidity and cooperativeness.'

35 Get Rich Quick, Get Smart Quick

The largest Ponzi scheme in history, orchestrated by Bernie Madoff, was exposed in 2008. The estimated losses were somewhere in the region of $65 billion. These schemes appear time and again in various forms, with different types of investment, often using new technologies like cryptocurrencies in order to lure unsuspecting investors. The story of Charles Ponzi and his scheme is a cautionary tale that warns of the dangers of investment opportunities that seem too good to be true.

You Only Have to Get Rich Once is the title of Walter Knowlton Gutman's 1961 book. See *The New York Times*, 30 April 1986: https://www.nytimes.com/1986/04/30/obituaries/walter-gutman-dies-an-analyst-and-artist.html.

On index funds, see Warren Buffett's 10-year bet against active investment management: https://www.finanzen.net/nachricht/etf/hedgefonds-geschlagen-warren-buffett-gewinnt-10-jahres-wette-und-zeigt-worauf-es-beim-investieren-wirklich-ankommt-5685785. Described in detail in Warren Buffett, *Letters to Shareholders 1965–2023*, Explorist, p.1878.

36 Ruminate

See: Johann Wolfgang von Goethe, *The Sorrows of Young Werther*, translated by David Constantine, Oxford University Press, p.5.

Another wonderful excerpt about brooding: 'Yesterday as I was leaving she gave me her hand and said, "Adieu, dear Werther." Dear Werther! It was the first time she had ever called me dear and it pierced me through and through. I repeated it to myself a hundred times and last night, getting ready for bed and muttering all sorts of things, I suddenly said, "Goodnight *dear* Werther" – and laughed out loud to hear it.' Ibid., p.78

Another superb novel about ruminating is Marcel Proust's *In Search of Lost Time*. The narrator, Marcel, is often absorbed in detailed memories of things that happened in the past and conversations that he analyses again and again. These past events are not only remembered but also vividly relived.

We mainly ruminate over interpersonal matters. Very rarely do we get caught up thinking about, for example, how we should have looked at the Matterhorn a little longer the last time we were in Zermatt.

37 Trade Your Reputation for Money

A more recent example than Gupta is Andreas Bechtolsheim, a Silicon Valley investor who, despite already being worth an estimated $16 billion, thought it necessary to engage in insider trading and ruin his reputation – even though he 'only' gained a profit of $400,000 as a result (an insignificant sum by his standards). See: 'In Silicon Valley, You Can Be Worth Billions and It's Not Enough', *The New York Times*, 23 April 2024: https://www.nytimes.com/2024/04/23/technology/andreas-bechtolsheimin-insider-trading.html.

Warren Buffett: 'It's insane to risk what you have': https://www.thestreet.com/investing/warren-buffett-weighs-in-business-economy-14500016. Although this is mentioned in the context of leverage, it also applies to corruption. The rare letters that Buffett writes to the CEOs of his companies are not to be compared with the annual letters to Berkshire Hathaway's shareholders. Those to the CEOs are not usually published.

Another personal anecdote: years later, when I'd started working on books, an entrepreneur offered me a million euros to write a sugar-coated biography about him. To have or not to have a million dollars! I wrestled with myself but ultimately turned him down, because biographies are outside my circle of competence. It was a lucky escape: years later, the entrepreneur ended up in jail. My reputation would have been in tatters.

Warren Buffett's 'newspaper test': 'We must continue to measure every act against not only what is legal but also what we would be happy to have written about on the front page of a national newspaper.' See: 'Warren Buffett's Biennial Letter', 21 March 2011, https://www.petefowler.com/blog/2011/03/21/warren-buffetts-biennial-letter.

On the subject of this grey area: ibid.

Another thing to add with regard to the fourth and final point: it's not just about you. Even if you personally aren't corrupt, steer clear of shady people. Sooner or later, hanging around with them is bound to rub off on you. Instead, band together with people who are better than you. Good company is the best guarantee for a good life.

38 Never Suffer

Keynote by NVIDIA CEO Jensen Huang at 2024 SIEPR Economic Summit at Stanford University: https://www.youtube.com/watch?v=cEg8cOx7UZk, time code 36:00.

Some people are born with a silver spoon in their mouth but find themselves facing difficult tests later in life. This is what happened to former *Washington Post* publisher Katharine Graham. Her husband cheated on her, suffered from bipolar disorder and took his own life. Later she was confronted with challenges at work, such as the Pentagon Papers, the Watergate scandal and a workers' strike that almost ruined the newspaper. She dealt with these crises, emerging stronger and even more brilliant than before. See *Katharine Graham: Personal History*, Knopf, reissued edition, 2002.

If the suffering is too intense, too crippling or lasts too long, there is no 'boost' to be had. Instead, this can lead to risk aversion, depression and a negative view of the world. Many Holocaust survivors, for example, have suffered from PTSD, depressive episodes and serious anxiety disorders. The trauma they experienced during the Holocaust often had a lasting impact on their mental health.

39 Let Your Emotions Define You

Thinking about the negative consequences that anger may have (e.g., damaged relationships, idiotic investment decisions, missed opportunities) can discourage you from acting under their influence.

This is known as a meta-study. Sophie L. Kjaervik and Brad J. Bushman, 'A meta-analytic review of anger management activities that increase or decrease arousal: What fuels or douses rage?', *Clinical Psychology Review*, Vol. 109, 2024,102414, ISSN 0272-7358.

Don't identify with your emotions, otherwise you'll fall into a self-fulfilling prophecy. For example, if you see yourself as an anxious person, you will actually become more anxious. Same goes for anger, envy and indignation.

40 Try to End It All

We are not particularly good at predicting our future feelings. See: https://en.wikipedia.org/wiki/Affective_forecasting.

41 Marry the Wrong Person – and Stay with Them

Germany has a divorce rate of around 30 per cent: https://www.bib.bund.de/DE/Fakten/Fakt/L131-Zusammengefasste-Ehescheidungsziffer-Deutschland-West-Ost-ab-1970.html. Switzerland's divorce rate is roughly 40 per cent (the author has contributed to it): https://www.bfs.admin.ch/bfs/de/home/statistiken/bevoelkerung/heiraten-eingetragene-partnerschaften-scheidungen/scheidungshaeufigkeit.html.

To find out more about why we cannot change people, see the following articles:

Hudson, W. W., & Fraley, R. C. (2015), 'Volitional personality trait change: Can people choose to change their personality traits?', *Journal of Personality and Social Psychology*, 109 (3), 490–507. DOI: 10.1037/pspp0000023. Summary: while this study primarily focuses on personality trait change, it also touches on the importance of compatibility in relationships. Compatibility involves alignment in personality traits, values and goals between partners. The research suggests that compatibility contributes to relationship satisfaction and stability over time.

Luo, S., & Klohnen, E. C. (2005), 'Assortative mating and marital quality in newlyweds: A couple-centered approach'. *Journal of Personality and Social Psychology*, 88 (2), 304–26. DOI: 10.1037/0022-3514.88.2.304. Summary: this study examines assortative mating, which refers to the tendency of individuals to select partners who are similar to themselves. The research suggests that couples who are more similar in various domains, including personality traits, attitudes and values, tend to report higher levels of marital satisfaction and quality.

Trying to change your partner is a waste of time. In the words of Charlie Munger: 'If you want to guarantee yourself a life of misery, marry somebody with the idea of changing them.' In Peter Bevelin, *All I Want to Know Is Where I'm Going to Die So I'll Never Go There*, PCA Publications, p.108

If you're planning to commit yourself, you'll need a lot of samples (dates) first. In the words of the investor Peter Thiel: 'If you decide to get married to the first person you meet at the slot machine in Las Vegas, you might hit the lottery ticket, but it's probably a bad idea.' *Wall Street Journal* video interview: https://www.wsj.com/articles/peter-thiel-competition-is-for-losers-1410535536, time code 5:00.

The secretary problem: https://en.wikipedia.org/wiki/Secretary_problem.

Never marry for money: Warren Buffett, *Letters to Shareholders 1965–2023*, Explorist, p.403.

42 Celebrate Your Resentment

An example from literature is Jean Valjean, the protagonist of Victor Hugo's *Les Misérables*. After many years serving an unjust prison sentence, Valjean meets the local bishop, who takes away all his pent-up anger and resentment.

The George McGovern story is a successful example of how to defuse resentment in politics: 'With rare exceptions, I feel strongly that McGovern's rule is an appropriate one for all of us. The longer I live, the more I observe that carrying around anger is most debilitating to the person who bears it.' Katharine Graham, *Personal History*, Knopf, reissued edition, 2002, p.604.

Charlie Munger on resentment: 'And that made me consider which of all the twenty Harvard School graduation speeches I had heard that I wished longer. There was only one such speech, that given by Johnny Carson, specifying Carson's prescriptions for guaranteed misery in life. I therefore decided to repeat Carson's speech but in expanded form with some added prescriptions of my own. ... Resentment has always worked for me exactly as it worked for Carson. I cannot recommend it highly enough to you if you desire misery. [Samuel] Johnson spoke well when he said that life is hard enough to swallow without squeezing in the bitter rind of resentment.' https://jamesclear.com/great-speeches/how-to-guarantee-a-life-of-misery-by-charlie-munger.

Here's another trick from the former British prime minister Benjamin Disraeli, courtesy of Charlie Munger: 'For those of you who want misery, I also recommend refraining from practice of the Disraeli compromise, designed for people who find it impossible to quit resentment cold turkey. Disraeli, as he rose to become one of the greatest prime ministers, learned to give up vengeance as a motivation for action, but he did retain some outlet for resentment by putting the names of people who wronged him on pieces of paper in a drawer. Then, from time to time, he reviewed these names and took pleasure in noting the way the world had taken his enemies down without his assistance.' In Charles T. Munger, *Poor Charlie's Almanack*, The Donning Company Publishers, p.71.

43 Join a Cult

Ideologies are consolidated beliefs: this is the core thesis of Daniel Dennett's book *Breaking the Spell: Religion as a Natural Phenomenon*, Penguin.

The Moonies: https://en.wikipedia.org/wiki/Unification_Church. Charlie Munger: 'How do you take a normal kid who is just a little miserable, take him off for a weekend in the country and turn him into a brainwashed zombie who, for the rest of his life, sells flowers on the street corner? ... It is obvious. It is a total lollapalooza. The Moonies achieve it by combining psychological tendencies to act in the same direction. There are about 20 standard tricks that can be used to trigger lousy cognition of that type. And the Moonies have figured out how to play four, five, six, seven, or eight of them at the same time ...' See: Chris Franco, 'The Charlie Munger Guide to Lollapalooza Effects', CMQ Investing, 13 January 2022: https://cmqinvesting.substack.com/p/the-charlie-munger-guide-to-lollapalooza.

Daniel Dennett quote: *The New York Times*, 19 April 2024: https://www.nytimes.com/2024/04/19/books/daniel-dennett-dead.html.

Property as fiction: you can dig over a plot of land as many times as you like, but you'll never find a scrap of paper with the owner's name on it. And yet we accept the convention that our neighbours' house belongs to them and not to us.

The fiction of global order: which constitutional global order should apply? The one we have today? The one from 1945? Why not the one from 1914 or 1815, or one from antiquity?

The fiction of human dignity: how does human dignity come about? And when exactly does it begin: during the initial contact between the molecules of the sperm and the egg, or not until the last of the three billion base pairs of DNA molecules have recombined? Against the seriousness of science and the truth, also see Paul K. Feyerabend, interview in Rome, 1993: https://www.youtube.com/watch?v=sE1mkIb1nmU, time code 6:00 ff.

On the importance of mockery and satire in this context: 'How much truth is contained in something can be best determined by making it thoroughly laughable and then watching to see how much joking around it can take. For truth is a matter that can withstand mockery, that is freshened by any ironic gesture directed at it. Whatever cannot withstand satire is false.' Peter Sloterdijk, *Critique of Cynical Reason*, The University of Minnesota Press, p.288.

44 Try to Change People

Another example from literature: the German writer Theodor Fontane explores something similar in his novel *Effi Briest*. The main protagonist, Effi, tries to conform to the strict social demands of the day. Her husband, Baron Geert von Innstetten, also tries to turn her into the perfect Prussian housewife. Despite her best efforts to be a faithful and well-adjusted wife, Effi is unable to suppress her youthful exuberance. The story doesn't end in suicide, but Effi does die lonely.

Charlie Munger quote: in Peter Bevelin, *All I Want to Know Is Where I'm Going to Die So I'll Never Go There*, PCA Publications, p.108.

Parents, teachers and even social media no longer hold the biggest sway over young people; their circle of friends and acquaintances, the people with whom they compare themselves most of all, are the biggest influence. Tip: try surrounding yourself with people who are better than you – you'll find that your personality will be lifted up. It also works the other way round. Psychotropic drugs are another exception to this rule – they change people's character too.

There's still the ethical question of whether we should be allowed to change ourselves or other people, even if we could. After all, a modified person ceases to be the same person. If I were to change my friend, for example, I would be erasing the person he once was. He would no longer exist. There would be some other person in his place. Even if I had obtained his consent before changing him, the new 'modified' friend might take offence at this personality alteration because the two of them are different people. Perhaps he'd terminate our friendship because he was no longer interested in being friends with me. Not to mention the repercussions this would have on and for his social environment. Derek Parfit (*Reasons and Persons*) and Thomas Nagel (*Other Minds*) have written extensively on this subject.

45 Say Everything You Think

Ingeborg Bachmann quote: '*Die Wahrheit ist dem Menschen zumutbar. Rede zur Verleihung des Hörspielpreises der Kriegsblinden.*' In: *Kritische Schriften*, herausgegeben von Monika Albrecht und Dirk Göttsche, Piper, pp.246–8.

Max Frisch and Ingeborg Bachmann promised to be completely honest with one another. See letter number 74 from Frisch to Bachmann, 29 June 1959, in: Ingeborg Bachmann and Max Frisch, Suhrkamp, *Wir haben es nicht gut gemacht*, p.129.

46 Spin Multiple Plates

Cal Newport, *Deep Work. Rules for Focused Success in a Distracted World*, Grand Central.

We could multitask successfully if we had two or more brains.

Sophie Leroy, 'Why is it so hard to do my work? The challenge of attention residue when switching between work tasks', *Organizational Behavior and Human Decision Processes*, Vol. 109, Issue 2, 2009, pp.168–81, ISSN 0749-5978: https://doi.org/10.10 16/j.obhdp.2009.04.002; https://www.sciencedirect.com/science/ article/pii/S0749597809000399.

47 Do Only Shallow Work

The terms 'shallow work' and 'deep work' are taken from Cal Newport's book *Deep Work. Rules for Focused Success in a Distracted World*, Grand Central.

Unfortunately, not all low-intensity activities are negotiable in life. We all have to accept a certain degree of tedium, especially in domestic matters and family life: shopping for groceries, mowing the lawn, cleaning, paying bills, all that dire sitting around in children's playgrounds.

Philip Roth quote: in Christine Kearney, 'Philip Roth reflects on novel's decline and "Nemesis"', Reuters, 5 October 2010: https://www.reuters.com/article/lifestyle/philip-roth-reflects-on-novels-decline-and-nemesis-idUSTRE6942MM/.

Ian McEwan on reading being 'at least as important as playing tennis': https://www.youtube.com/watch?v=KBrCngwREXg, time code 2:53.

Bill Gates' extreme concentration: in Cal Newport, *Deep Work. Rules for Focused Success in a Distracted World*, Grand Central, p.257. Also the examples for Teddy Roosevelt and Peter Higgs.

No one wrote more poetically than Mary Oliver about focus and attention: 'This is the first, wildest and wisest thing I know: that the soul exists, and that it is built entirely out of attentiveness.' In David Brooks, 'The Quiet Magic of Middle Managers', *The New York Times*, 11 April 2024.

48 Invite Bad People into Your Life

'Give a whole lot of things a wide berth': in 'A Conversation with Charlie Munger and Michigan Ross (Ross School of Business), 2017': https://www.youtube.com/watch?v=S9HgIGzOENA, time code 40:00.

On the mother who gives her son two sports shirts: Paul Watzlawick, *The Situation is Hopeless, But Not Serious*, W. W. Norton & Company, p.81. Another example from Watzlawick:

'the wish for a particular gift and the disappointment when one receives it "only" because one stated that wish', ibid., p.93. Also: 'Say or do something that another person could very well interpret either seriously or humorously. Depending on his reaction, you can now accuse him of either ridiculing a serious matter or having no sense of humor', ibid., p. 83.

On the subject of zero-based affection: 'Warren [Buffett] is humanly wise, too, so naturally I began to share with him things in my private life. His comments always helped. One day I called him because I had been hurt by a friend. "Don't forget," he told me, "she has zero-based affection," meaning that you always had to start from scratch, with no reservoir of goodwill or of love.' In *Katharine Graham: Personal History*, Knopf, reissued edition, 2002, p.604.

'… we would rather achieve a return of X while associating with people whom we strongly like and admire than realize 110% of X by exchanging these relationships for uninteresting or unpleasant ones.' In Warren Buffett: *Letters to Shareholders 1965–2023*, p.445.

49 Go Where the Competition is Strong

Buffett quote: CNBC Warren Buffett Archive, https://buffett.cnbc.com/video/1998/05/04/buffett-the-secret-of-life-is-weak-competition.html, time code 01:00.

Jennifer Doudna quote: in Walter Isaacson, *The Code Breaker: Jennifer Doudna, Gene Editing, and the Future of the Human Race*, Simon & Schuster, p.6.

Competition is for losers: based on Peter Thiel's talk at the Stanford Business School: https://www.youtube.com/watch?app= desktop&v=3Fx5Q8xGU8k&t=837s, time code 37:00.

Also from Peter Thiel: 'If you want to create and capture lasting value, look to build a monopoly.' See 'Competition Is For Losers', *The Wall Street Journal*, 12 September 2014: https://www.wsj.com/ articles/peter-thiel-competition-is-for-losers-1410535536.

Canadian business thinker Roger Martin is one of the world's leading experts in strategy.

Henry Kissinger quote: https://www.goodreads.com/quotes/60 9695-the-reason-that-university-politics-is-so-vicious-is-because.

Two bald men and a comb: in Leander F. Badura, 'Zwei Kahle und Ein Kamm', *Jungle World*, 23 June 2022: https://jungle.world/ artikel/2022/25/zwei-kahle-und-ein-kamm.

50 Say Yes to Everything

The tip to imagine that the request is for tomorrow came from my friend Guy Spier.

Warren Buffett plea to his employees: in Peter Bevelin, *All I Want to Know Is Where I'm Going to Die So I'll Never Go There*, PCA Publications, p.52.

The five-second no originally comes from Charlie Munger: 'You've got to make up your mind. You don't leave people hanging.' In Janet Lowe, *Damn Right! Behind the Scenes with Berkshire Hathaway Billionaire Charlie Munger*, John Wiley & Sons, p.54.

The Irish author George Bernard Shaw reacted rather undiplomatically to invitations. His response to an invitation from the West Edinburgh Labour Party: 'It would be easier and pleasanter to drown myself.' See Letters of Note: https://news. lettersofnote.com/p/i-decline-to-sit-in-a-hotroom-and.

The second reason why we are reluctant to say no is FOMO, the fear of missing out. This fear is completely unfounded. There are millions of things that could (and are going to) happen to you. A couple more or less won't make any difference. What's important is that you say 'yes' to things that are actually aligned with your goals.

Seneca quote: in Maria Popova, 'The Shortness of Life: Seneca on the Busyness of Life and the Art of Living Wide Rather Than Living Long', *The Marginalian*: https://www.themarginalian.org/2 014/09/01/seneca-on-the-shortness-of-life/.

51 Crowd Your Life with Gadgets

The research on this is clear. Cornell professor Tom Gilovich is a leader in the field.

James Hamblin, 'Buy Experiences, Not Things', *The Atlantic*, 7 October 2014: https://www.theatlantic.com/business/archive/ 2014/10/buy-experiences/381132/.

Marie Kondo, *The Life-Changing Magic of Tidying Up: The Japanese Art of Decluttering and Organizing*, Ten Speed Press.

52 Fall into the Content Trap

Number of tweets on X: https://whatsthebigdata.com/twitter-statistics/#.

And this only concerns content produced by human beings. Before long, AI will be generating reams of amazing stuff.

Another filter: content behind a paywall often undergoes stricter checks than free content, which may be tainted with advertising, prejudice, propaganda or obvious errors. So be mindful of where your information comes from. And beware of synthetic traps. AI-generated content is going through the roof, making it harder and harder to distinguish between real insights and clickbait created by algorithms. Stay alert. If the content appears too personalized and too perfect, be *very* careful.

Epilogue

Matt Ridley, *The Evolution of Everything: How Small Changes Transform Our World*, Harper Collins, Position 3733, Chapter 14.

Warren Buffett on the subject of role reversal: 'I would also always ask, "If our roles were reversed, what questions would you ask me if I were running your business?"' In Peter Bevelin, *All I Want To Know Is Where I'm Going To Die So I'll Never Go There*, PCA Publications, p. 164.

Richard Thaler: ' … . using these heuristics causes people to make predictable errors. Thus the title of the paper: heuristics and biases.' In Richard Thaler, *Misbehaving: The Making of Behavioral Economics*, W. W. Norton & Company.

Rolf Dobelli is a Swiss writer, novelist and entrepreneur. He has an MBA and a PhD in economic philosophy from the University of St Gallen, Switzerland. He is the bestselling author of *The Art of Thinking Clearly*, which became an instant bestseller, has sold over three million copies worldwide and been translated into 40 languages. Dobelli is also the founder and curator of WORLD.MINDS, an invitation-only community of the most distinguished international thinkers, scientists and artists.